NEW AND SELECTED POEMS

First published in 2007 by
Dedalus Press
13 Moyclare Road
Baldoyle
Dublin 13
Ireland

www.dedaluspress.com

ISBN 978 1 904556 83 1 (bound)
ISBN 978 1 904556 84 8 (paper)

Dedalus Press titles are represented
in North America by Syracuse University Press, Inc.,
621 Skytop Road, Suite 110, Syracuse, New York 13244,
and in the UK by Central Books,
99 Wallis Road, London E9 5LN.

Printed and bound in the UK by Lightning Source,
6 Precedent Drive, Rooksley, Milton Keynes MK13 8PR, UK.

The Dedalus Press receives financial assistance from
An Chomhairle Ealaíon / The Arts Council, Ireland.

NEW AND SELECTED POEMS

Pat Boran

ACKNOWLEDGEMENTS

As well as previously uncollected poems, *New and Selected Poems* includes work from the following collections: *The Unwound Clock* (1990), *Familiar Things* (1993), *The Shape of Water* (1996) and *As the Hand, the Glove* (2001), all issued by The Dedalus Press under its then publisher, John F. Deane, to whom sincere thanks are due for his support and encouragement over the years. A small number of poems were originally included in the chapbook *History and Promise* (IUP, 1990).

New and Selected Poems was first published in 2005 by Salt Publishing UK: my grateful thanks and continued good wishes to Chris and Jen Hamilton-Emery. This new Dedalus Press edition includes a very small number of additions and revisions, most of them in the earlier part of the book where, despite my resolve to let things stand, warts and all, a few lines seemed to cry out for assistance. Though I was tempted to add more new poems, I allowed myself only two I had overlooked in making the prevous selection.

Acknowledgements and thanks are due also to the editors of the following in which some of the new poems in this volume first appeared: *The Stinging Fly* and *The Oxfam Poetry Calendar 2005; Sunday Miscellany* and *The Living Word,* RTÉ Radio 1. 'Bread' was commissioned by Eoin Brady at Lyric FM, set to music by Elaine Agnew and first performed by the National Chamber Choir, under conductor Celso Antunes, at the National Gallery of Ireland in September 2004.

Contents

≈

from *The Shape of Water* (1996)

from *As the Hand, the Glove (2001)*

ix

New Poems

Reading Pat Boran

Introduction by Dennis O'Driscoll

Pat Boran describes Portlaoise, the County Laois town where he was born in 1963, as 'our once congested, now double-bypassed town'. Following EU-funded 'bypass' operations, midland towns like Portlaoise are no longer clotted with city-bound traffic. The conference hotel where tight-suited insurance men endure a pep-talk from their regional manager; the shopping centre beyond the church where stubbly farmers, on the way home from a mart, stock up with tea bags and fruit cake; the pallid public hospital: all have reverted to local phenomena. The *Shell Guide to Ireland* judges Portlaoise to be 'noteworthy merely as the location of the Republic's only male convict prison'—thus sentencing the town to be bypassed by potential visitors also (except, of course, the involuntary kind).

Portlaoise would have been largely bypassed by literature too, were it not for the fidelity and clarity with which Pat Boran has portrayed the town in his work. County Laois may mean little to the tour guide whose coach passengers are intent on chalking up a sighting of the world-renowned Rock of Cashel rather than the locally-cherished Rock of Dunamase, or to the executive whose digital organiser burns with the urgency of his next city appointment. But, for those who inhabit the town, it is the centre of the known world. Here they are: the schoolboy who grows drunk on the wine uniform of the girls' school; the widow parking 'her black Raleigh / outside Whelan's butchershop'; mourners 'escorting / a body down the street'; 'the square, / a country town, neighbours / stripped of their professions and their trades, / aprons hung and blinds pulled down, / the accordion band doing its best'. And what is a town without its characters? Eddie Boylan of the grocery shop on Lower Main Street is recalling his youth (a 'fading world, rich / in an obsolete currency'); the Guru Maguire achieves instant celebrity on a TV chat-show; Hannigan's brother 'went to the dance and never / came home again'; a mischievous delivery man is ferrying chickens in a van with '*wash me* back doors'.

Vividly though the moods and mores of his small town world are captured, there is far more to Pat Boran's poems than what he terms 'footnotes to a local history'. It is not just that, like all good poets, he universalises experience but also that his imagination ranges freely, responding to everything from Dublin street scenes to celestial mysteries. Diverse in theme, wide in scope, modulated in rhythm, his poetry excels at making what Seamus Heaney calls the 'transition from the world of data to the words of invention'. That Pat Boran would become a poet in the first place seemed almost preordained from the moment in his youth when—proving that the Muse moves in mysterious ways—brochures for the family's travel agency in Portlaoise came packaged with a tour of Miroslav Holub's work:

> One of the first poems to make an impression on me was Miroslav Holub's 'A Boy's Head'. Possibly more than any other, with its great endorsement of the imagination, it marked the beginning of a physical (in the sense that it came from outside my own geographical world) and a mental journey into writing. And the fact that I first came across it on a printer's offcut from some anthology which had been used to wrap brochures for my father's travel agency was poetic in itself.

Perhaps it is to the example of Miroslav Holub, a scientist as well as poet, that Pat Boran owes one of his great strengths—an objectivity which might be described as scientific; an ability to maintain a determined detachment from his subject-matter, to distance his poetical 'I' from an empirical self in order to gain a clearer perspective on the world. Yet his detachment is in no way doctrinaire; tonal warmth and emotional empathy are always on hand where appropriate to a love poem or elegy. Apart from the scientific stance it often adopts towards reality, Pat Boran's work reflects a keen interest in scientific thought itself. Names overheard in his books include those of J.B.S. Haldane, Niels Bohr and Albert Einstein. There are 'Notes Towards a Film on the Life of Galileo Galilei'; an eclipse of the moon is observed through a poetic lens; and 'Bedtime at the Scientist's House' suggests that the raw facts of scientific data cast a story-like spell ('Tell us the names of Jupiter's moons, / the valencies of atoms 1 to 103'). In the poignant 'Waving', childhood recollection unexpectedly segues into scientific epiphany at the precise moment where a cloying note might have been a danger.

When experimenting in his own language lab, Pat Boran—never afraid to risk fragmentary utterances—is more often a poet of implication than of explication. The reader works backwards from the evidence presented as frequently as the writer moves forward towards a final click of narrative closure. From the very start, he triumphed at one of the hardest calls in poetry: gauging when to regard a poem as finished and best left alone. He never overstates or overstays; the poems are remarkable both for their resonance and their restraint. Viewed very broadly, Pat Boran's work falls into two principal categories: poems which chart the human struggle to make sense of our existence on a mysterious planet afloat—maybe even adrift—in space; and those in more direct mode where people are recorded in life, elegised in death or celebrated in love. In the latter mode, he could as justifiably have named his second collection *Familial Things* as *Familiar Things:* the familiality displayed in poems about parents and siblings breeds unsentimental tenderness, as in 'Song for my Parents':

> Evening sky and age, you do not take them,
> but rearrange the furniture of home
> until they lose themselves among familiar things.

Eight years later, in the tightly-crafted *As the Hand, the Glove*, the familiar things are themselves lost: the old family home is as empty as the shells of the wave-washed 'House of Shells' in his first book ('the tide in its gables almost audible'). The wireless 'breaking out into the world beyond / our sleepy, listening midland town / in a house since vanished' is described as 'the only thing on earth defined / by absence...Wire-less'. The defining absence in *As the Hand, the Glove* is that of the poet's recently-dead father whose 'disappearing act' prompts questions that can never be answered and quests - of recovery and discovery - that can never be fulfilled. Pat Boran writes evocatively about childhood and children. 'Children' is a piercingly perceptive poem, one of his very best; he writes well too of childhood icons like Desert Island Dick, of a 'breezy, childhood room made infinite / by conspiracies of movement and light' and of an ostracised, bullied child.

A preoccupation with time, its ravages and ramifications, is what draws together the thematic threads of his poetry - personal and scientific, local and global. The meagreness of the human life-span is all the more evident when set in the continuum of infinity and space. Even language cannot be relied on to preserve what is being lost to ageing and dying: 'We feared speech / knowing of the alliance / between language and time'. In the opening lines of 'Am', a poem in memory of his father, a watch-face mirrors his own face:

> 1.35 a.m.
> I look at my watch and see
> my life story:
> I thirty-five am...

Somewhat older than thirty-five though Pat Boran now is, his poetry is not at all as well-known or widely-read as it deserves to be. It would be an overstatement to describe him as neglected—his poetry has, from the first, enjoyed the admiration of his peers; he also gained recognition as children's author, festival programmer, editor, reviewer, broadcaster, workshop director—but he is undoubtedly underrated. Hence this attempt to briefly encapsulate his poetical oeuvre as a whole (and not just the selection from it he has made for this book); and, while almost as sceptical about introductions to poetry volumes as I am about cover blurbs, I feel impelled to make a sole exception in this case because of my longstanding conviction that Pat Boran's work merits a large readership and serious critical attention. His absence from many anthologies too is surprising, given how satisfying his poems can be not only collectively but individually (think of 'Song of the Fish People', 'Literature', 'Machines', '"The Dead Man's Clothes"', 'The Immortal' and numerous others already cited).

Several years ago, I found myself riveted by a short story set in London and read on the radio (or should I say 'wireless'?) by an actor. I had missed the beginning of the broadcast, and had absolutely no clue as to the author's identity; yet I quickly realised that he or she had writerly skills in abundance. Discovering later that the story was by Pat Boran, I was confirmed in my view that—even on a blind tasting—here was a writer whose talent for language was unmistakable. Perhaps the fact that I had entered the story at its half-way stage was telling in itself: he is a master of writing that plunges its audience *in medias res*. 'It's like what happens with water' his third collection, *The Shape of Water*, blurts out with buttonholing bluntness in its first line, not even pausing to remove its sopping hat and hang up its raincoat. Now himself *nel mezzo del cammin*, the timely selection published here allows us to savour a cross-section of Pat Boran's finest work. Author of a chapbook called *History and Promise*, he is also a poet of mystery and fulfilment, of the eternal and numinous no less than the earthly and everyday. Although a spirited celebrator of the local and the known, he steps 'beyond / the porch-light of language' to hazard the dark and comfortless unknown.

from The Unwound Clock (1990)

House

Water clanks from the tap
like a chain—a lifetime

since anything has moved here
but rats and birds. I see

the last inhabitants as a father
and son, the father

sending the son off to the city
with a handshake and a pocket

of old pound notes.
He might as well be sending him

to bring home the time
without a watch to carry it.

For a Beekeeper

You rise in the morning, the residue
of dream-honey on your eyelids.
Mornings you are not at your best, but then
facing breakfast you remember how
the wings of your bees beat *how many
times a second?* how flowers are identified
by a sense more akin to taste than smell
or sight ... You see the queen,
big like a fruit, the precise
network of the honeycomb, the flowers
like excited shopkeepers, opening
their shutters to the sun's gold coin.

There is barely time to shine your shoes
when, already at the window, the first drone
beckons you to court.

House of Shells

Before Kildare there was water.
Before the town rose from the ocean
the spot was marked by occasional rocks,
sea-rounded hillocks, and birds which flew
patient circles overhead.

2

Slowly it began to appear
and the places that would become Melitta Road
or Bride Street were tiny rivulets
draining off into the sea.

Crude homes were built of stone,
and for the first time strings of smoke
trailed like kites in the sky.

3

When the last drops of ocean
had rejoined the seas or risen to the clouds
Kildare got on with the business
of being a town,
and any intimacy with water was forgotten.

So complete was their forgetting
they would maybe go to Bray on holiday
or travel west to marvel where the Barrow passed.

4

Then as they slept one night
the ocean, wishing to refresh their memories,
threw a huge wave-wash across the town,
leaving a house of shells,
the tide in its gables almost audible.

Widow, Shopping in Portlaoise

She parked her black Raleigh
outside Whelan's butchershop
and bought her brother his chop.

The basket creaked with meat.

She orbited the roundabout
in the Market Square
and stopped there for bread

where a brown dog tore a refuse bag.
The cream on buns
yellowed in the sun
and tinsel paper caught dead flies.

A fridge purred the pleasures of a 99.
To "How's all at home?" she replied
"Fine" as if it were a brand name.

And then she cycled home again the pothole road,
breathing like an old engine,
whistling as she came through the gate exhausted
to see her brother shout abuse at a hen.

Guitar

for Kate Stewart

Music came from behind his fingernails
where the day's dirt was. A hint of face
was visible in his round red beard.
An organ grinder ground to a halt
to listen as the music came
from the tramp's broken silhouette.

And the monkey slowed down to a Viennese waltz.

Soon the street had frozen to a painting:
the baker had stopped baking, the butcher,
bejewelled in a chain of sausages, imagined
the melody drifting delicately down the street
like soap bubbles blown by the old guitar.

Seahorses

for Michael Boran

The oceans of our world were barrels:
three or four of them, driven in
like straying cows under cover
of nightfall, scoured out with a strong
jet of water from a hosepipe rigid
with a sense of duty, and left there
for the rain to fill while the hose
withdrew innocuously to a shed.

Full almost immediately in memory,
those oceans fulfilled their doubted promise:
we used their water to splash our Ford
Consul to a semblance of cleanliness,
launched our rubber band and lolly-stick-
propelled troop-carriers on their images;
I think my sisters even dipped
their tresses in those perfect portraits.

All that they lacked was life—as yet
outside of our abilities, though over-
flowing from our imaginations. So much so
that quite a time had passed before
we recognised the tiny specks,
transparent brown, the shape of those
blind-spot question marks that glide
a fraction behind the point of vision.

In marmalade jars we scooped them out,
astonished by their resemblance
to the seahorses of American comic book
advertisements.
                              Believing they had
come from rust, I dreamed of pushing
our tired old car into a real ocean,
crossing the waves on seahorseback, eating
nothing as an adult but marmalade.

The Tulip Evangelist

You knew if Fr. Brown
had visited O'Connors
from the perfume of tulips
that he wore.

O'Connor was a flowerman
who swore sap flowed
in his veins, and his tonsured head
was itself a peculiar bloom,

petals of grey hair pushed
behind protruding ears, or drawn
with Brylcreem smooth
across his dome.

When the priest had eased
his conscience with two or three
large, slow pots of tea,
he would leave the cottage,

dream down the single-street town,
astonished bees searching him for stamen,
real tulips in the convent garden
becoming giddy as he passed

as if they had looked into
a Mirror of Scents, and found
in that black cassock
brilliant images of themselves.

The Castlecomer Jukebox

We often travelled to Garryhinch for turf,
my mining-town father and I,
kissing the wet road

in his lip-red Volkswagen van.
The song on his lips was always
Play To Me Gypsy—"beside

your caravan". How has it happened
that this is his only song?
Outside Kilkenny in two rooms,

eight boys and their six sisters
rearranged the contents of a home, and grew,
approximately, into each other's clothes.

Did they all have just one tune—
something popular in their youth become
the soundtrack for their lives?

A haiku-worth of *Play To Me Gypsy*
recorded by him in that house
with the outside toilet.

December, they stood side to side
or in a perfect vaudeville arc,
smiling, snow and stars outside.

And their parents, uncommonly relaxed,
crunching home-baked cakes like popcorn, tossed
a thrupenny bit giddily, hand to hand,

whispered together like teenagers,
selecting the Christmas Dinner song
from their barefoot Castlecomer Jukebox.

Return of The Castlecomer Jukebox

And even if we listen to ourselves so much
we hear nothing of the world about us;
and even if our pockets are always empty
and our calendars full of disappointments;
there will always be some youngster, wiser
by our foolishness, with a coin he has kept
for just the right time—when the dancing
has stopped and the jukebox light is gone out.

Homecoming

I'm happy to accept.
His route will eventually
deliver me to my destination,

and the sunlight
presents a landscape
of artistic definition.

At Timahoe (the house
of St. Mochua) he stops
to fill his truck with chickens.

The flask of tea offered
in return for my assistance
is whiskey. "Hitching?

There's always a hitch."
He laughs as I lift
the twentieth plastic tray.

Then his draining swig
and a pigeon inspecting
our casual work,

and he, unawares, shutting her
into our mobile tomb
with the epitaph *Irish Chickens.*

2

Petrol stations and pubs
comprise the greatest part
of our meandering,

and at every stop
his humorous philosophies
flow like the refreshments.

In Stradbally (the single-
street town) he picks up
a girl in sailor suit, fifty

odd miles from the sea,
has her singing *Michael Row
The Boat Ashore* in minutes.

I can think of nothing
but the pigeon—an unwilling
Jack Kerouac of the bogs—

silenced though I am
by expectation
and some magical feeling.

3

At Portlaoise (the fort
of Laois)—my stop—
he pulls up gently,

busy dazzling the girl
with his wit, absently
shakes my hand

and lights them both
courting cigarettes.
While they smoke

I quietly open
the *wash me* back doors,
and a thousand chickens,

nervously ecstatic,
excused by death
from the restrictions of gravity,

burst unstylishly
into the late afternoon sky
in the guise of a pigeon.

Camden Street in the Morning

Camden Street in the morning, and a man
lifts a piano above his head,
emerging for a day he knows will offer
only rain and criticism:
You eejit, Paddy.
Eight hours of this await him
with reporters asking:
Can she be really worth it?

Even so
what do they know of his nights?
that tower of pianos silent to the moon?

Master

Drummer with a country & western band,
he was master
of the standard dowel.

Like a martial artist his arm became
a rope of steel:
I am no style

and I am all styles. Breath.
Then that polished blur
across my fingers,

snare, high-hat, snare, high-hat,
tom-tom, timbal,
side, bass, kettle drum
                    & cymbal.

Strangers Buried Him

The farm was in his palm
a map complete with fields

the buckets to be scrubbed
spotless, all those gates to shut

the brook the bream were found in
known solely to himself

perhaps a dog or two
and the curate from the village

Wheat rippled on his skin
birds built their nests in him

and that first black Morris Minor
was ditched there somewhere

advising hasty retreat to those
who salivated over foxes

2.

Strangers buried him
(family by credentials)

seeing nothing—not even
the contour lines of sileage heaps

printed on his cutlery
as they packed the past in tea chests

and argued about
the most direct route home

The Cartographer's Son

1.

The world is on its head:
with uncanny accuracy
and their new-found power
apples fling themselves at trees
returning from the dead.

The world is on its head:
dust and insect droppings first,
sweepings of the bower,
sucked up by the sudden thirst
of time roused from bed.

The world is on its head:
birds are up all night.
Oblivious to the hour
they track the sun's erratic flight
until their wings are lead.

2.

Blood rushes to the brain:
the waterfall draws its cool tongue
of bubbles and spray
up a cliff face, lichen-hung,
to a rendezvous with rain.

Blood rushes to the brain:
badgers, fieldmice, red ants
dizzy on their way,
struggle through their exhausted dance
of twigs and sprigs and grain.

Blood rushes to the brain:
happiness is a gas
he inhales as he plays,
down on hunkers with the hour-glass,
subverting time again.

The Cartographer's Assistant 2

I awake
as my alarm rings
(someone about to say
what I already know.)
I deal with these things
brutally.

～

The car leaps daywards
over stones, pools,

cattle-grids ...
Rain thumps the roof.

The radio—
louder than everything.

～

"Yes, what is it?"
his secretary greets me

(the most efficient salutation—
Company Directive.)

Yes, what is it, Ms Jones?
Yes, what is it, Mr Jackson, Master Shore?

～

Just lately I've begun to find,
weekends mostly, whenever I

relax, doctor,
there's a ringing in my ears,

and if I lift the phone:
heartbeat
                    birdsong
                                        rain ...

The Man Who Became What He Ate

For dinner he is facing
a brilliant silver fish:
diamonds of light bathe him,
cast a portrait in darkness
across the ceiling, the shadow
of some huge submarine
gazebo.

      She comes pulling on
great wings, circling over him,
her eyes like blinding headlights,
takes him in her talons
to her breast, and soars
through clouds—rotating
capons on a spit. He has never
known such wind.

      And far
below, distorted by the ripples,
the fading fingerprints of event
on water, he sees himself,
or someone—with knife and fork
in that blue room, his girlfriend
stretched across to kiss
his puckered lips.

His First Confession

Had she come to me with crimes
I'd heard before, or even
crimes unknown (for instance

computer fraud—a novelty
yet to reach this parish),
I would gladly have exchanged

the most insignificant
of penances—a running
genuflexion in the aisle ...

But today the grille and darkness
seemed more for my protection
than presupposed Gothic

decoration. Nine years old,
in finery of First Confession:
I hate you, Father.

The stone more silent
than it's ever been, daylight
flooding through the doorway.

Cities

We build our cities close to mountains,
for this: so that in brilliant sunshine
we may crawl and claw to the summits
to look out over the magnificent
transience of what we are.

The Living Room

A onetime philatelist I'd kept the glass,
never one to allow anything which brought
the minute into view to pass.

Enthusiastic and in my prime,
I'd magnify the tiniest mass
ten, a hundred, a thousand times.

Huge were the rings of wood, the whirl
of fingertips, the amoeba's mime.
Still, the lure of something minuscule.

When the glass failed, my will
persisted towards the molecule,
the atom magnified to fill

a cathedral, angels singing around
electrons, protons, the invisible
neutrinos. Even still, these sounds:

a candle sputtering in the gloom,
a fly declining solid ground,
you chuckling in the living room.

The Guru Maguire's Journey to the Centre of the Earth

When his moviestar penpal died
old Maguire received an invite
to appear on television and reminisce.

A taxi came to his home, its door
outstretched for a handshake,
and it took him to a great fortress

where, after a quarter century
of celluloid clips, the toupeed host enquired
whether anyone might like to relate

some personal memory.
Maguire was still, his eyes
averted from the lights

in which he saw, ghostly,
the faces of all the greatest
Hollywood idols, totally numbed

by such inane chat shows.
"Her calligraphy," he said,
"was like plant life in repose."

During commercials the car reappeared
to take him back to his little street
where his neighbours waited up with tea,

flooding the street with their revelry:
"So how did it go, Mickey?"
and "Is it really a toupee?"

Living With Artists

Toby gradually died;
a leg was powerless,
his blind eye shed white tears.

They put his dish in a plastic bin
and fixed the gate where every day
he'd etched his image in the paint,

barking in vain his strange language
to misunderstanding schoolkids.
There had been a time

when the least event would send him
bounding towards his oeuvre—
a low triptych on the kitchen door

or his uncompleted fresco after Goya
in the chicken shed, long since
without the patronage of fowl.

But then the years passed
in cruel sevens,
roughing up his eye,

stealing his once precise retention.
His autumnal passing remained
unmarked by publication,

broadcasts of interviews
or toasts in artistic circles,
while a pocket-sized mongrel

moved into his studio,
scrutinising the fresh paintwork,
nervously attended by my mother.

Concert off Kensington High Street

By ten o'clock the site was alive:
Casey, the foreman, already chewing on his pencil,
a kettle boiled for the first strong teas,
and Cookey on the mixer had prepared
a wonderful cement that made the men's mouths water.

High up in the scaffolding
Big Bill sang the blues,
balanced delicately on an old black bucket
that doubled as a piano stool.

By noon he had finished the wall,
tinkling the ivory bricks into place
with so passionate a history of Basin Street
that Casey made a collection among the crowd
in a riddle, directing latecomers from the street
with his No Parking megaphone
to the less desirable, cement-bag seats.

When You are Moving into a New House

When you are moving into a new house
be slow to write the address in your address books,
because the ghosts who are named there
are constantly seeking new homes,
like fresher students in rainsteamed phone booths.

So by the time you arrive with your books
and frying pan, these ghosts are already
familiar with that easy chair, have found
slow, slow creaks in the floorboards,
are camped on the dream shores of that virgin bed.

American Juggler on Grafton Street, Dublin, October 1988

Quiet as Bohr's
celebrated model of the atom,
the balls seem held there
in space and in time
for our scrutiny.

Even the raindrops
are reluctant to fall
before such understanding.

"Start young," summarises
an old voice, not unwearily.

Perhaps in the laboratory
with a handful of electrons
after school is out?

Have You Left Mountmellick for Ever?

Old yellow hut at the end of the garden,
jet sprays aerosol foam on the sky:
Have you left Mountmellick for ever?

The convent has me drunk on wine
uniforms, Maguire's dog snaps a trap
of teeth through their gaudy fence.

Have you left Mountmellick for ever?
The Christmas tree is still up—in April—
just a naked spear. I expect to see

the shrunken head of Christmas
or you continually zebracrossing to make
the boys in leather jackets grit their teeth,

stamp their cigarette butts out and cry,
gulping back years of lust and tears:
Have you left Mountmellick for ever?

The Immortal

I'm Martin Drennan from Ballydavis,
tipping back glasses of Guinness
and whiskey in Dinny Joe's,

remembering the balls in the town hall
where I'd slip in unnoticed
to watch and drool

Woodbine ash from the balcony.
And out in the Market Square,
fresh with the smell of pigs,

before the Wright brothers
changed the dreams of men—
long before spluttering aeroplanes—

those arms of empty haycarts
looked like antiaircraft guns
aligned, jutting into sky,

and the spit-and-polish farmers,
always gaunt in monochrome,
scrutinised the camera

that captured for posterity
their endangered species—
the Irish between wars.

from *History and Promise (1990)*

Coins

Capt. Ger Grant of Moyne, Co. Tipperary, a highwayman, was the last person to be hanged in the Old Gaol, Maryborough (now Portlaoise), in August 1816.

He would bathe in streams,
tiny fish at home around his limbs,
eat nuts and berries by the road,
shave with a lake for his mirror.
Woods and forests—his friends—
concealed him in comforting arms.

Or so freedom seemed
in his memory.

But this country had been taken from him,
as once he had taken its precious coins,
draped in shadow on boreens where
lone horsemen sauntered between towns.

And in place of the streams they had given him
darkness, and the tantalising smells
of Maryborough women
baking bread in turf stoves.

Finally they gave him a noose to wear
and, closing his eyes, he was back in a landscape
of wood and stream as autumn issued
its first, water-marked leaves.

Small Town Life

My neighbours escort
a body down the street,
a woman enclosed
with clothes—the first
and last gift of society. Wreaths
hint towards a relationship
between death and beauty,
as the mannequins,
their eyes open, dream
in the windows of a department store,
wearing the clothes we say we would die for,
and in which, any day now,
we may be buried.

The Flood

Mrs. O has made a grotto
of her window ledge, saving first
the statue of the Virgin, followed by
a print of uncle John in '63,
a birthday card in crayon
from her nephew, her lilac blouse
and a jewellery box already rusting.

The boats that pass before her
have been disentangled from
the overgrown back gardens
of this nightmare Venice, this mockery
of the honeymoon she never had.
Oh that there had been time for uncle John ...
Oh that Seamus Brennan had come back for her as promised ...

Where are they now as the waters level off
and the boys in waders help to drag
the furniture outside? Now that the house is empty,
save for the smell of damp that will never leave.
Now that she must find another place to go—
having already packed for what she thought
would be her next and final departure.

A priest with a bucket slops about next door.
A local journalist photographs a fish.
Someone calls her name, but she ignores it.
History has returned to her midland town,
three hundred years after Cromwell's men,
and she is alone to face the interrogations.

Memorandum

Many earths away is where I was
yesterday, last year, is where today
I am headed. To find myself

I must open the doors and windows,
front and back, like a schoolchild
look both ways before the road.

For always I am on this string
of being—unformed—somewhere
between history and promise.

Lower Main Street

i.m. Eddie Boylan

I remember your room and the table,
and your brother hovering about in the background,
the knots of knuckles in your fingers,
the way you eyed my cassette machine with suspicion.

But I do not remember exactly how I came to be
close to you in your final years, to coax you
back to when you were my age, a boy
in a turn-of-the-century midland town

where newspapers were the post-communion liturgy
at the back of church. And in the richness
of tea and grain, scents I did not recognise
then, nor have I since, we faced each other,

young men across a century of change, our town
outside your grocery shop transformed at such a pace
that, stepping out from your fading world, rich
in an obsolete currency, the notes

for that article in my hand—only
the butcher's greeting made me real in time
as the clocks of his hanged carcases dripped
seconds on the slab behind the glass.

Forest

The forest is a sleeping hedgehog,
stars are watching a big scrub-brush hill
and a lump of stone.

You'd miss the sound of the cannons
that destroyed the spot I'm standing on.

Dunamase, 1984

I Know This Road

I know this road, these trees, that moon
over Dunne's cowshed. I have approached
with these same steps outside of dream.
It is a place kept for a time
when all else might be saved—countless
replicas of Dunamase, Drowning Fish
T-shirts, the light and shade of village streets
by village artists, talk, the harvest—
all but that moon, these trees, this road,
footnotes to a local history.

A Lover's Graffito

And what if all that surives of here—
        this squinting, twisted town of ours
        with its fortress prison and barricades,
        its three-storey street with two abandoned
        to storage space,
        the littered square,
        the motorway,
        Gandon's ruin,
        the new estates—

is this shed with the door kicked in,
a cider bottled, our scribbled names?

Alternative Histories

What would we do if all the historians
were found dead, their voices silent,
their theories, illegible,
stuffed in their pockets?

When I was twelve the only man
who knew who built the fence around that field
was discovered face down in the barley,
his last words lost on crows.

And if we know this morning
who lives in this or that house, who owns
the corner shop with the paper stand,
we are unaware of the wind outside,

the chimney-pots shifting ominously
on their perches, the fast cars coming
blindly into the bends ahead, driven
by historians who have yet to learn our names.

from *Familiar Things (1993)*

"Let me enter the history of the world,
if only to hold an apple"
—The angel Damiel in Wim Wenders' *Wings of Desire*

Night

for Larry Cosgrave

Night, fog, ice on the road,
the town spirited away in this cloud
to where, just hours from now,
at dawn, with only our imperfect memories,
we must begin again, rename
the birds, the streets, the songs—in short,
all that we have known and would return us,
love permitting, to an image
of this earth for ever.

Waving

As a child I waved to people I didn't know.
I waved from passing cars, school buses,
second floor windows, or from the street
to secretaries trapped in offices above.
When policemen motioned my father on
past the scene of the crime or an army checkpoint,
I waved back from the back seat. I loved to wave.
I saw the world disappear into a funnel
of perspective, like the reflection in a bath
sucked into a single point when the water drains.
I waved at things that vanished into points.
I waved to say, "I see you: can you see me?"

I loved 'the notion of an ocean' that could wave,
of a sea that rose up to see the onlooker
standing on the beach. And, though the sea
came towards the beach, it was a different sea
when it arrived; the onlooker too had changed.
They disappeared, both of them, into points in time.
So that was why they waved to one another.
On the beach I waved until my arms hurt.

My mother waved her hair sometimes. This,
I know, seems to be something else.
But when she came up the street, bright and radiant,
her white hair like a jewel-cap on her head,
it was a signal I could not fail to answer.
I waved and she approached me, smiling shyly.
Sometimes someone walking beside her might
wave back, wondering where they knew me from.

Hands itched in pockets, muscles twitched
when I waved. "There's someone who sees me!"
But in general people took no risk with strangers,
and when they saw who I was—or wasn't—
seemed relieved, saved from terrible disgrace.

Now it turns out that light itself is a wave
(as well as a point, or points), so though for me
the waving is done, it's really just beginning.
Whole humans—arms, legs, backs and bellies—
are waving away, flickering on and off,
in and out of time and space;
pushing through the streets with their heads down,
smiling up at office windows,
lying in gutters with their kneecaps broken
and their hopes dashed; driving, loving,
hiding, growing old, but always waving,
waving as if to say: "Can you see me?
I can see you. Still ... still ... still ..."

Latin 1

Like some minor general's, my Latin
was a bellicose affair: either *Veni, vidi ...*
or *Omnia Gallia in tres partes
divisa est.* Though I might know myself
(and, in a rare extrapolation,
think and therefore be) I could not
avoid the squadron drills,
the legion obstacles placed before me.

But consolation was not far off.
Without such necessary expressions as
'facing unemployment'—its own sure fate—
the language could prove good only for history.

Latin 2

What did Latin ever do for you? What good is it?
I asked my mother, as she stood to listen patiently,
detergent suds clanking on her wrists.

I'd have none of it, or it would have none of me,
my precious hours spent instead on languages
still living, and some new-born—the litanies
of rock music existentialists and saviours.

I called an end to wars for such exotica.
My mother must have felt the same, there in that kitchen,
her head a marvel of connected words and meanings
which, when I paused, I still could wonder senseless at.

And Latin beneath us both, like a blanket of bog
through which little living, and nothing of any value, might emerge.

I'll Do It Again

Auld Lang Syne drifts up from downstairs.
Norma Desmond is lying on her bed,
wrists bandaged, her would-be lover
by her side to hear
her first resolution of the year:
"I'll do it again. I'll do it ..."

2.

Again and again my father boomed
(pointing to broken glass,
spilt milk, or turned,
drained of colour, to the sky
where my brother's expletive still drifted
offensively towards ...)
"Will you do it again?"

My brother's predicament—
everybody's then—
was how to sound compliant
with a negative verb. As it happened
all that issued from his lips was
"I'll do it again".

3.

Again and again, in places
brought into being only through
volition or resolve, MacArthur returns,
the sinner repents, the alcoholic
walks into the clean light, clean, shaven.

While, elsewhere, the failing Hollywood actress
thrusts herself into imagined spotlights,
and generation upon generation of ghosts
sifts through immaculately remembered homes,
hopelessly trying to do it all, or undo it all, again.

Born to Shave

I'm so tall now at 28
the only thing I see is my chin,
the place where my head becomes lost
in my clothes and might be anybody's.
I look for myself in this mirror
and find only a chin, sometimes
a tooth, occasionally my tongue.

And so I wet my invisible face,
like someone blind apply, blindly,
the foam—resisting the chemical smell
until it dissipates—and bend my knees
an inch or three so that I know
it is me that I am shaving.
Born to shave.
                        A child
looking in the same mirrors, I saw then
only ceiling, followed, years later,
by hints of hair, then eyes,
and then this chin. Born
to age and shave.
Born to grow up to face myself.
Born to regret and, in the light
of regret, to make promises, like this:

Years from now I'll reach
from some otherworldly place,
where none of this means anything, to touch
this hand-basin, these dulled blades.

4th September, 1991

60

Children

Children in ill-fitting uniforms
drive adults to school, and children
argue the cost of tobacco
in the Newsagent's nearby.

You must have noticed them.

And in the mornings they rise to slaughter pigs,
cook breakfast, solve crosswords at the office ...
Or they send tiny adults into minefields,
barefoot, with pictures
of Khomeini around their necks,
their old toes searching the sand
for death.

And children queue for Bingo
on Ormond Quay, on Mary Street,
and douse their leaking take-aways with vinegar.

And children talk and smoke incessantly
in Eastern Health Board waiting rooms,
always moving one seat to the right,
someone's parents squabbling over trinkets
on the worn linoleum.

And it is always children
who will swear for their tobacco—children
with beards and varicose veins—
and children, dressed as policemen,
who pull their first corpses from the river.

And who is it who makes love in the dark
or in the light, who haunts
and who does all our dying for us,
if not children?

We leave their fingerprints
on everything we touch.

Always Books in your Room, Margaret

Yet the books will be there on the shelves, well born,
Derived from people, but also from radiance, heights.
—Czeslaw Milosz

Always books in your room, Margaret:
I met Chaucer at your bedroom door
years ago. While dodging school
we faced each other an hour or more—
his language a foreign place.

Always books in your room, Margaret:
Yeats and Kavanagh stayed behind
awhile when you went off to college,
bearing—they never seemed to mind—
the lack of direction in my face.

Always books in your room, Margaret:
the feeling I had on Sunday drives
when you were home was that we shared,
though silently, in countless lives
across the world and down the years.

Always books in your room, Margaret,
and, little by little, books in mine.
Like the suburbs lurking in Coughlan's sandpit
when we were small, which, in time,
found language for their hopes and fears,

the suburbs growing in my head,
populated by the real, the dead,
the imaginary, understand they owe
a debt to you. And their wish, so:
always books in your room, Margaret.

Fathers and Sons

One night recently, da,
you may not remember,
you told me you believed your beard
was growing backwards —
two, three days of growth
disappearing.

You were tired, but in good form,
almost excited, slipping
from the shadow of yourself.

We laughed for different reasons:
you, on hearing your claim aloud
as if it were a stranger's—
a frightened laugh
that still believed in magic—
I, remembering the story
of my brother's son, aged 4,
nicking his downy cheek
with daddy's razor.

Song for My Parents

They're at home now, looking out at the evening,
hearing the floorboards creak, the distant
hum of factories. The town, the house
they hoped to pass to me, has changed.
The small routines of favour
to one butcher rather than the next
are fading. They forget
what they were about to say, and why.

Evening sky and age, you do not take them,
but rearrange the furniture of home
until they lose themselves among familiar things.

Notes towards a Film on the Life of Galileo Galilei (1564-1642)

1. Personal Detail

One of history's
only major figures
remembered by his given name.

2. Scientific Method

In the absence of anything better
used his pulse as a standard
against which to make his measurements.

(The more exciting he found the work,
the more inaccurate were the measurements.)

3. Opening Scene

Galileo, frustrated for years,
compresses his whole being
into one expectant eye
which his new telescope
fires into the night sky.

Like a comet trailing awe
he runs down stone spiral stairs
into a courtyard of marketing peasants,
their stalls scattered
in a wild constellation of wares.

Bedtime at the Scientist's House

for Peter

Tell us again how the universe contains
no straight lines, though Saturn's rings
stay coin-thin to 500,000 miles.
Tell us that one again.
We always enjoy it.

And tell us the names of Jupiter's moons,
the valencies of atoms 1 to 103.
Illustrate constant random motion,
quasars on the brink of invisibility.

Show us, oh please, the picture
of a space-time world like a medicine ball
dropped in a net. Just once more,
softly, like music,
then we will sleep.

The Past

When there was little time
we ran.
Everything monitored us,
measured our progress.
Clocks beat in our chests,
beneath our feet;
and there were slower clocks—
the clouds, the planets.
We feared speech
knowing of the alliance
between language and time.
And so we ran
until we had exhausted
time and ourselves.

2

How long are we here now?
Days? Years?
Always listening.
Every now and then
we watch ourselves
run past or collapse in tears.
It would seem there are only
beginnings. The past
is not erased, but drawn
in the sweep of hands
over the clock face.

After the Trial

There's a flash of blood
across his cheek—a thorn perhaps?—
and his eyes seem to watch from somewhere
other than where he stands. "Yup there!",

shouts the father; "Yup!", the son.
The father's stick breaks on flesh
and he swears, as does the youngster,
at this dumb beast.

The old man grew up on the road
between the mart and farm.
He got his first taste of mortality out here
one evening driving milkers to a shed.

Nothing above or below ... He's earned his rest
and the right to ignore the ancient fear.
He'll accept a lift to town, and drink,
while his son starts up the tractor,

wipes his hands, and takes the road home
all his lifetime strewn with dung.

Modus Vivendi

Forget the future, your death,
the surprise on your face. Forget
everything you'll learn, too late.
Arrest the thought. What could compare
with the selflessness of plants
that mark the spot
where you will lie? If such
unthinking things can justify
the presence of the sun and planets
more completely than can you
(with all your grave considerations),
why think at all? Why squander
the irreplaceable energies? Abandon,
like some evolutionary cast-off,
this thing that brings us closest
to extinction. Forget the evidence,
the argument. Close your ears
to all debate. Forget I ever said a word—
forget this poem.

The Crow

Drive faster; you can still see the hills—
blossom of honey, burden of unfound gold.
A line of trees, like an army on manoeuvres
searching fields, swings towards the road
but misses; the hedgerows and gates you hung on,
pissed at, or cupped her tiny breasts beside,
are run one into the other, blurred by speed.

So drive. Only a crow is motionless in his sky,
burning there like the opposite of a star
over that which may be left, but not forgotten:
your mother pulling curtains on the world,
ashes of toys drifting in the yard,
the back of his hand across your face,
the distance to these hills.

The Voyage

for Liam Brady

The terror is, everything's important.
I hope you're used to constant interruption.

You might, for instance, decide to bring a stone,
an old worn shirt, perhaps a favourite sonnet.
But were you with her when you found that stone
or wore that shirt? And didn't you read that sonnet
once, towards the end, to see her tears?
You understand now something of the difficulty?

Such questions come to you unbidden.
It's a hell of a place for a man to be alone,
and here we are, still within sight of shore,
and our thoughts already turned to love and poetry.
Mea culpa. So much for resolutions.

2.

You have stopped to consider before we sail,
before the ship pulls heavily out into the darkness—
portholes full of crescent moons, the creak
and groan of rigging ... But then again, I suppose
you've read the brochures, met others back
from other haunted journeys down the years.
You know as much as any what to expect:
a spot where suddenly the wind may fail,
the ocean freeze over to a glass,
abandoning you to your own devices

for what may seem like years, and be! Or
you'll be beset by demons, monstrous gargoyles
conjured from the emptiness of space—
everyone you ever knew or loved!
Oh, you may. Nothing is ever certain.
(Every day's a May Day here, believe me.)

3.

So, tell me, am I right: it is a woman?
Be warned in advance, do what you will,
you won't forget her. It's all been tried.
Be like the fish who float below the surface;
resist the lure of nightly apparitions,
the desire to cling to things you should let pass.
Remain in darkness, darkling, that's the ticket!

4.

The ship itself? Facilities? As you can see
the swimming pool's unused and strewn with litter.
Travellers seldom come out here to exercise
for better futures. Or to dine. Toilets
are down on either side—starboard and port—
railed off, to be precise. You catch my drift?
Fresh water, I'm afraid, is strictly rationed.
You'll probably notice that from time to time
aromas will come wafting from the kitchen—
roast beef, duckling, caviar—anything
from Indian cuisine to Irish stew.
The cook just looks right through you if you mention it.
You'll find him by his empty pots and almost

taste his longing, see his gnarled hands peel
the ghosts of onions in his lap. And he
is not the most afflicted, not by any means.
Though there be many dark and lonely hours,
invoke the Lord and thank Him lest you too
prove to have such recollective powers.

Who else? The minor author, yonder, haunted
by even more minor characters than himself
who, bent on plain revenge, whisper "Excuse me"
over and over for days, "Just fine" or "Thank you,
do call again"—the toneless voices, not of death
but of all those whose lives amount
to next to nothing. "Call again. Do-do-
do call again." But as I've said,
you'll know them soon enough for yourself.

5.

So—*Pullmans, loos, the rigging and the mast,*
Moby Dick, the seven-headed beast,
swab the deck, go easy on the beer,
and no more talk of you-know-who from here
on out... That must be it. Excuse the doubt,
but it isn't every day we're into port—
the noise and music, carnival of what's real,
first sight of smoke from chimneys makes you feel
like smoke yourself. You find you cannot touch
the yearned-for flesh. What is too much
is to be frightened by a woman's charms,
to run away, to flee the harbour's arms ...
But when you're out at sea you can describe
in perfect detail that first and precious kiss,
the clothes she wore, the magic in her eyes.

If you should pass me on the deck you will not miss
the signs of an unearthly presence which,
though many years ago now—more than your own—
has never left me. Many bear the mark
of dreaming. Oh to be a busy man.

But you'll remember where you left those keys!
The telephone numbers of everyone you know!
The boys in the band, the football team ...
Films you thought you hadn't even seen!
You'll be amazed how quickly you'll adapt.
In a week you'll swear the sea and present company
of ghosts and dreams was all you ever had.

Safekeeping

In the dream-land of a child
I met a man who would never die,
to whom could be given precious things.

But the map was lost, or the child was wrong.
The eternal man was never found.
Hard wind is the only wind that sings.

I leave my gifts in this snow for you
where I lose myself, trying to be true,
following footprints—probably my own.

A Life

Accumulating;
that's how I survive the emptiness.
This speaks, that demonstrates;
a stack of books taller than myself
can not be done without,
remembers in detail
all the things I cannot face,
at least just yet.

But it might end now, this hour, this minute.
That may be a casual birdsong I hear, but this
my causal breath. Even the woman I love,
she whom I seemed to meet
just in time to save myself, so recently,
even she is not here in this moment
to which my whole life may have been leading,
and from which everything may lead for her, alone.

So what of all this stuff? I invest
against the odds, even now, feverish,
on my back. I cannot ask
for immortality, but words
belong in time, record a love
of life, of living—and relay the shock
that everything is as I had suspected:
the dream of someone other
than her or me, something we stumbled into,
wide-eyed, pinching ourselves, to embrace
among useless possessions.

Dark Song

Here we are in the park
with darkness crouched behind trees
and daylight dissolving over the city.
Something unbelievable is happening.

All day this ghost of knowledge
has whispered in my ear, all day
the very cracks in the footpath
seem significant. Something unbelievable ...

The meteor of your cigarette tip
swoops close to earth, hearth
of loving in a cold universe.
The playground swings grind their teeth

and pause. What else is there to say?
It is in our silences now, as in our voices,
that something unbelievable.
We are growing older.

Angels in Love

When angels fall in love
they dance on the heads of pins,
throw themselves into fireballs, or stay
underwater in the pool for hours.

Sometimes they even slash at their wrists
with razor blades or wood planes,
failing, of course, to tear the delicate skin.

For, in the absence of pangs, or flutters,
how else would they emulate our love?

Seven Unpopular Things to Say about Blood

1
Our mothers bled, and bleed,
and our enemies,
and our enemies' mothers.

2
It rushes to the finest
nick, romances the blade.

3
It dreams
the primary dream of liquids:
to sleep, horizontally.

4
It is in the surgeon's heart,
the executioner's brain.

5
Vampires and journalists
are excited by it; poets
faint on sight.

6
I knew it better as a child,
kept scabs, like ladybirds, in jars.

7
Blood: now mine would be with yours
until the moon breaks orbit
and the nights run cold.

Fireworks

The sky in darkness.
Silence throughout the entire city.
The present moment
so close it might be touched ...

And just when we might endure no longer
above our heads they explode:
momentary stars, flowers of light
against the darkness.

2.

This night in childhood, in the square
of a country town, neighbours stripped
of their professions and their trades,
aprons hung and blinds pulled down,
the accordion band doing its best
for dancers and drunks—no fireworks then
but the flash of a camera in the crowd
the flare of matches, our beacons
of belonging and continuum.

3.

The intervening years gone in a flash.
All changed and nothing ever changed.
The gathering of tribes, the merging
of lives and histories in appointed moments.
As bells rings out the old and in the new,
tonight again we sing as time itself
like some flower of light explodes.

The Museum of the Near Future

In the museum of the near future
we walk around the exhibit of ourselves,
lips pursed, bent on stiff legs
to view the exposed undersides.
"Well, you seem to have gained a little weight,
though, yes, it probably is the light.
But what can I be thinking of—
those awful sideburns!" Never mind,
ours is a dance of cursory inspection.
Once we notice there's a party in the next room,
the thrill of being our own guests, of sticking
fingers in our own future wounds, wears off.
In moments we're like tourists without plans,
or manners, drinking all we can hold, stubbing cigarettes
into the carpet because, look, we won't be back!
And hey, if that security guard is leaving.
we could make love right here, right now,
next week's edition of *The Irish Times* beneath us ...

Thrown out for causing a disturbance,
we stand in the rain, incredulous, soaked and sober,
shoelaces undone, our flies open,
the museum behind us impossibly grey.
"Are you ok?" You just can't help laughing:
"What was all that about?" you ask. We kiss.
It's hard to say, looking at your perfect face
and the already fading scars I glimpsed.

Internal Aeroplane

Like the man who built an aeroplane in his garage,
full-size, completely functioning (well, almost...),
like that man who then could not get it out of there,
in my heart is every detail of our future,
and it pains me to sit still even for a moment,
and we pass each other suspiciously on the stairs—

you wondering what all the carry-on is about,
trying somehow to maintain composure
in the face of such tormented sorcery;
me, feeling wingtips against my ribcage,
my breath smelling of aviation fuel.

Today, perhaps, I might concede:
there was sufficient space outdoors, and daylight
could only have been a help to failing eyes.
But for every dream we launch successfully
into the skies, countless, flightless hulks
rust away in hangars of the heart.

Since You Left ...

the days have learnt a new language,
evenings speak in tongues—

the voices of rain at the bedroom window,
of wind whispering in the rain-swept street,

the house pipes calling,
bowl to water bowl.

Loss discovers new songs
in ancient instruments.

Love

1

Nothing making sense
but love
in the space where space should be
all that's expected.

2

Nothing right
in the heart of things,
the body of things,
prowling in the rain.

3

Love: the watchmaker
sleeping, his invention
loose in the world.

from *The Shape of Water (1996)*

If I were called in
To construct a religion
I should make use of water
    —Philip Larkin

one's not half two. It's two are halves of one
    —e e cummings

Entrance

It's like what happens with water,
a lake, for example,
which you open
slowly with your hands,

when you sigh, unintentionally,
at a concert recital,
and the breath seems
inseparable from the pain:

you're made human again.

A Revelation

A persistent nibbling sound
coming from the socket by the bed,
as if electricity were a mouse
gnawing away in the dark. So up I get

and, afraid to throw the switch, strike a match
then stretch out on the floor to come face to face

with what I am and have been since birth—
positive and negative in equal parts,
the yin/yang drama of my troubled heart
ignorant of but dependant on the earth.

A Confession

Since none of this makes sense,
since memory is a rope,
since you and I are blind,
I have to confess:

I walked. When I thought
the earth at my feet
was a road, I walked
till I came to the shore

and spent the night there
listening to water,
exposed to starlight
millions of years old.

2.

Winter was a child burial,
spring a silent meal,
summer
a room full of distractions.

For how many hundred years
have painters turned to a vase like this,
to the light filtering through petals
to describe the world?

Renoir's and van Gogh's
simple flowers in a simple bowl.
You are painting now, again,
to fill the space.

3.

In the early days I too
chose silence. It seemed, at first,
more honest than forcing words
after which—more silence.

But these last few nights the door stands
open between opposite worlds:
one in which I am still your man
and content to be,

but another in which an unnamed boat,
untied from its mooring rope,
drifts out of harbour
into uncertainty.

For My Goldfish, Valentine

Such enormous sadness
in such a tiny world.
And, looking down at you
in the water clouded
by your flaking scales,
I wonder if my impulse
to take you home
last Valentine's Day
(following a goldfish dream)
was not just the desire
to share my tenancy
of these dusk-facing rooms
under winter's hold.

That dream of gold.

You can imagine how it took me
back into my own smaller body
and bigger, child's imagination
when I found you too incarnate
in an earlier form.
As the lama recognises
his master in a child,
entering the pet shop,
I knew you then at once—
the golden fish who swam
in the lens of my parents' house,
in the lens of my childhood,
before floating up one day
to leave that world as I
too left that world, as you
soon once more must leave.

Today in the meantime
you look out at me
with the same bewildered eyes,
mouthing the same mute syllable,
the eternal Om that says
nothing changes.

Lead becomes gold and gold lead.
A child will be god when god is dead.

Soon I will recognise your replacement.

Credo

I believe in a moment where things
come into themselves and everything
before and after is a kind of fading.
I believe, most days, in words
(as I might in diamonds) but
I try them between my teeth before I buy them.

I believe in truth, insofar
as it is a word with an almost
infinite number of synonyms
(though I can seldom think of any
and, when I can, am inclined to think
they're probably just something I've invented).

On a more sanguine note
I believe I may be dangerous
(to myself as much as to others),
inclined as I am to self-belief—
and this despite the evidence—
though when alone I'm known to compromise.

I believe in making deals,
in foreign influence, new ideas,
in changing minds, too—my own especially.
I believe in love and sex
and children, if they believe
in me. But this could be wishful thinking.

Truths and Rights? Well, these few here
appear self-evident, as they say:
life and the various pursuits.
Otherwise known as loss.
This I believe the ultimate truth:
the liberty to permit oneself to lose.

In the roundness of the planet
(for practical purposes), in life and art
as electromagnetic waves across the surface.
Of something unknown. This I believe.
And in this planet in my absence,
despite Berkeley's seductive philosophy.

In the future, therefore, though English
has evolved no tense for it
as if somehow doubting its existence.
So it would seem that I believe
against the odds, against words.
But I believe. Witness my belief.

I believe in things other,
things external, in history,
but in something like its opposite too:
a time unmeasured by events,
where clocks are works of naive art
like milk bottles left out beneath the moon.

I believe in a kind of Zen that says
dim the light to find the stars,
and in the little doll, the pupil, of the eye.
In rhyme, sometimes. I like the slow
almost wary fall of a word to its echo,
but I also like half-pairs, surprise—

And yet some warning might have helped
to make it easier when you left
last week. Though equally it might not.
If life's a relay, not a race,
doesn't that somehow help to explain
why progress is so often felt as loss?

Always back to loss. Still I believe
it is the handshake that makes the best
and most positive symbol of the human
(though I also rate the kiss
and, in recent times, the Mexican wave;
superstrings, not cause-and-effect chains).

In short (and what else is there?)
I believe the only real prayer
is a list, not of requests but of beliefs;
and this phenomenon of naming
is just another form of breathing
that reminds me how to *be* and how to *leave*.

The Sea

Mermaids on the rocks,
sirens from the shore,
and a bird's dark shadow
cast over the sea.

I am out again on the sea.

And it is out here the octopus wrestles
with air, out here red crabs
scuttle round in circles,
demented ticket-checkers

going nowhere. And then the quiet,

the sea like silk being torn
as the bird wrenches his new prey
out into sky. It must mean something
that this is how we dream the spirit leaves.

They Say

The gun dog stole his master's gun
and tried to bury it in the garden,
which might explain the noise.

For something woke the entire household
eventually bringing the master himself
from his book-lined study in his nightshirt

and hob-nailed boots—somnambulist
of the quiet hours—clutching air
then stepping out, cautiously,

cautiously, beyond

the porch-light of language.

Words

The answering machine
meets my arrival
with unblinking eye.
No word. Now even your voice
evades my traps.

❧

Fintan the goldfish,
recently bereaved,
swims round in his world
of light, transparency,
searching for his shadow.

❧

Turned sideways, the books,
face to face, square up,
insisting on their versions
of the same old story:
your life, my life.

❧

The wine-coloured bedspread
contoured like an ocean;
the wind in the trees;
and your absence ... These nights
I flounder not swim.

❧

The *pièce de résistance?*
Has to be this cup
with your lip-prints on it,
a tea-leafed shell
I hold to my ear.

≈

Calling your name
in laneways only alcohol
knows the way back to.
Every cat knows you now.
Wild dogs remember me.

≈

The hearth is always bare
in portraits of the Virgin
to signify virginity.
In mine a fire rages.
I'm burning your love letters.

≈

My clothes on the floor,
my body in a twist,
my heart turning over and over
the same old question: whose
words are these anyhow?

≈

The keyboard and mouse.
Or this old journal and pen.
At last, if only with fingers,
with fingertips, I'm feeling
for you again.

Moon Street

It's a minute to, a minute past,
but always the night of the sky,
the waxing or waning or full moon
here on Moon Street,

where every key fits every lock,
every heart is open or broken,
and posters of missing household pets
turn the railway station into a gallery

of loss. What's there to lose?
Come on, there's a party tonight.
Music waits to be released.
The windows are large enough to view

whole sweeps of sky, whole dusty
constellations too long swept aside.
Birds are singing when you arrive,
dancing, or exhausted, in Moon Street.

2.

In Moon Street when you meet she cries,
not on seeing you, but on not seeing
herself, as if a cloud had passed over
some taken-for-granted sphere, leaving

an inexplicable absence in the cosmos,
a strange wavering of otherwise perfect orbits.
But always you can feel that pull,
like the sensation of crossing someone's grave.

Moon Street. Could have called it
Ex-Girlfriend Street, but didn't.
Who could live there were there not
at least some small respite from ghostly visits?

3.

To give oneself completely
isn't wise. But wisdom isn't in it.
More footsteps have taken you to Moon Street
than dreams have shown you moons,

because you get there not by dreaming
but by walking in the wind or cold, or calm,
sometimes having washed, more often than not
ragged, worn and tired. You never realise

where you are going until you get there,
where nothing is planned, nothing is known,
and you're drawn back into the heart's old orbits,
tiny as a grain, massive as a moon.

A Creation Myth

The story goes that Wheeler stepped outside,
as is the rule. Great physicist or not,
when you're having dinner at Lothar Nordheim's
you find that leptons, bosons, quarks and whatnot

tend to dominate. It's a relief
when someone suggests a party game. "The door,
Mr Wheeler. Twenty questions. I believe
everyone knows, as it were, the score."

Laughter. Wheeler's exit. A puff of smoke.
(I always imagine him smoking in the yard.
Great physicists or not, we're all plain folk
in sudden darkness where any light's a star

and stars mean company.) But what was he thinking of
as it dawned on him they hadn't called him back,
and time was fizzling out like the red dwarf
of his cigarette fading in the dark,

leaving him alone there with his god?
Or just alone ... Time to go back inside.
Yet, as soon as he stepped in, the room seemed odd—
though it might have been the fact that he'd been miles

and years away, and now had to begin
all over, like some astronaut returned
to planet Earth and to these strange beings
who were, he knew—he told himself—his friends.

"Is it animal?" No. "Vegetable?" Well, he'd begun
at least and, in the beginning anyway,
the others answered normally, but then one—
a colleague—faltered, couldn't seem to say,

for sure, yes or no, as if somehow
she didn't know herself! And that smoke again.
Now it doesn't take a physicist to know
when something's not quite right. Still, being trained

in logic means you don't like to concede,
so by the time he asked, "Is it a cloud?"
he already knew that's what it had to be,
and nothing else. And even as the crowd

composed itself, themselves, and started to explain
their little joke—how they'd agreed not to consult
but just to play by ear—for Wheeler it was plain:
the expectation determines the result.

Desert Island Dick

He was a cartoon character
in some comic years ago,
bearded, scrawny, desperate,
but with no place to go,

obviously, except around.
Which is precisely what they did,
those footprints in the sand
that might have belonged to someone else

had they not led to where he sat
beneath the only coconut,
the only palm tree,
the only sky. One childhood night

I actually became him,
looking up at the stars,
listening to the ocean
of the only words I could remember—

no *Oxford English Dictionary,*
no Shakespeare or Bible then—
just the names of imagined characters:
my own, my family's, my friends'.

The Non-Existent Knight

after a painting of the same name by Tony O'Malley

I'm three, or thirty maybe, but the dark
is a breezy, childhood room made infinite
by conspiracies of movement and light,
refusals of the elements to work
their promised magic. Until the sun comes up
the world remains a curtain drawn across
my eyes, a veil across the nothingness
on which the only light cast comes from us,
from memory—that inner world which burns
but never dies.
                        Then here he is,
conjured in all the shades I've grown to miss,
in temporary, shifting, brilliant forms,
reborn in space and time to share this dust,
the patron saint of all my windmills lost.

The Guide

A dog in my dream.
I bend down to pat him
on the head, I bend down to
what-my-own-name-is
him on the head, but he steps
forward on what appears to be
the gravel path we're on

and my arm must extend
to reach him, and my feet
behind me on the ground
leave the ground
behind.
       Below.
                     Just inches first,
then a couple of feet, my feet,
above the ground, above
the moist perfumed secret earth,
and me floating face-down, stretched out,
limbs like a star's, like the turning
horizontal light the spirit makes
when the chakra doors are open, are free,
and then
            he starts to run,
scarcely moving at all at first,
(the way the best guides set off,
brisk enough to inspire confidence,
slow enough so we're never lost),
turning to check once in a while
that I'm there, here, following still,
to check on the state of my progress
with weightlessness.

And, having checked, he goes ahead
as only dogs can really go,
all curiosity, all zest for life,
like Neruda's dog on the Isla Negra,
bounding, bounding, bounding... And I fly,

above him, beside him, back up river;
I fly from the mouth towards the source
following my reflection in the water;
through reeds and rushes, sedge and moss;
under great then ever smaller bridges,
cathedrals of pure quiet, I go
half angel now myself, half spirit,
I fly. Then feel my flight slow

and find myself in deep woodland
where a handful of men in uniforms
stands beside a freshly-dug grave
in which two naked lovers, limbs
wrapped around each other, groan
in their labours, writhe and groan,
the dogs of earth howling for its moon.

The Prayer-Jar

At the bottom of the prayer-jar
was a layer of quiet
so thin it could be missed,
so quiet it might be worn to church.

At the back of the church
you could take, unseen,
the prayer-jar from your pocket,
to collect the sound of people shuffling,

and then go shuffling off back home
through the market visited earlier on,
the clucking of vendors and birds on perches
already somewhere in the belly of the prayer-jar.

Song of the Fish People

Give us legs and arms
to run and fight and kill,
then give us other skills
to plant and farm.

Give us warm blood
to feel the variations
of temperature, the patience
to untangle bad from good

while the known world spins,
and give us the desire
to create, and the fire
to destroy. Even take the fins.

But leave us always tears
that we may not forget
the salty depths
of our formative years.

The Shape of Water

Four days without it and I'd be dead
and yet I almost never sing its praise
(great evolved life-form that I am) while this shell
washed up on the shore does nothing else.

Like the search for meaning, the search
for the shape of water reveals
only the form of my enquiries:
a bowl, this boat, my body ...

Even when I cup it in my hands,
trying to see it for what is,
it takes my own shape, if temporarily;
it gives my own reflection back to me.

So, though we're intimate in the moment,
it seeming to know me as no other,
if water is what I love most—
this thing that has and is my measure—

it is because it sets me free,
because it has no memory.

Precipitation, evaporation, condensation ...
home to home to home ...

Blue planet the astronauts brought
home to grey cities and green fields;
blue eye of the quest for knowledge
turning in the heavens; blue, blue,
the planet Earth, which is really the planet Water,
a raindrop in the light of distant stars.

You are a distant star, my father
as a young man, and yet your light
persists in the eyes of this old joker
who sits opposite me across the table
where his precious brown-handled knife
lies beside the bread he's always favoured,
sliced, as always, down the middle so that air
might grant it the resistance he admires.

You, too, are a distant star, my mother
as a young woman, and yet your light,
projected as an image of you strolling
with your five children along the promenade
at Tramore (the long beach) shines still
more than a quarter of a century later
in the eyes of this woman drifting off to sleep
in the flickering lights of fire and television.

The boy on the sand
is king of the castle
till the sea takes it from him
and leaves him a man.

Clepsydra,
the water clock:

precise
forgetting.

⁓

Tradition says the inhabitants
of Eket in north Calabar
have a sacred lake,

and that the fish
of that sacred lake
protect their souls.

Perhaps it is
that humans
can not be trusted.

⁓

Among Greenland Inuit
spear heads are kept
in seal-shaped boxes

so that, when thrown
in the seal hunt,
they will know the way.

Inside the flesh
of the only fish
I've ever caught:

the smell of ocean,
the taste of ocean ...
and the hull of a boat.

⮑

Asked to reveal itself,
water says:
                     well,
that noise on the roof
as you sobbed in your beer
and damp wood hissed
and spat in the fire;
last night, remember?

Or, years back, years
ago, the arc
of a 6-year-old's piss
spattering leaves
at the edge of the forest ...

Listen, says water,
you can't become
an ocean
without first being rain.

⮑

My mother's tears at the hospital
when my sister's quartet of new-borns,
Kate, Sarah, David and Aoife,
commenced their ancient, wordless song;

my father's tears at his brother's funeral,
the bucket of clouds in the back yard,
the saucepan of water left out for Miller,
my uncle's dog with the blind eye:

great telescopes and simple mirrors
water leaves everywhere
to show the connections between things,
to show us what we really are.

⁖

Rain falling in sheets,
pages from the *i ching*
or Book of Changes;

small streams
gathering into rivers,
then heading for open sea;

water itself, never still,
never done, the mystery,
the greater part of me.

from *Miscellaneous Archival Material;*
Boran, Patrick G.

1. Main Street, 1971

I put the flashlamp into my mouth
and I am god or one of the gods
glowing with an orange knowledge
my human cheeks can scarcely contain.
Pumpkin-man, Volcano-Boy.
My head given a whole new life.

And so I know from experience,
how difficult it can be for gods
to speak lest they cremate the world.
Knurrege an ahvish nus de—sorry,
Knowledge and advice must be
imparted very carefully.

But who then put all those big words
in that leather-bound book my parents keep
in the sideboard of the sitting room,
a mouth of fire locked with a key?
God? Repeating himself like a drunk!
Or humans like me with flames in their mouths,
fire in their hearts and they burning to tell
the wonder of it, the loneliness of it.

4. Main Street 1996

There's a child on that hook
outside the butcher's shop
every time I pass, a child
dangling like a cup
from its handle.
                    I can't quite see
if the old block inside is gone
or what became of the ceiling-high
refrigerator since they hung
net curtains on the windows
and retired.
                    But someone forgot
the child on the hook outside,
the only thing
about this street that hasn't changed.

5. Why Clocks?

Because the house is a clock,
because every room keeps
time of a different period—

the dark room, childhood,
the living room, teenage;
infancy and old-age, hidden.

And I remember, too, a clock
where a wooden man and woman
came out when the temperature changed.

'Who's there?' they would say.
'Me,' I'd reply, a young man
still unused to these ancestral spaces,

rooms where a turkey
dripped from the neck
into the same basin each Christmas,

or where mice set off traps
in the still of the night,
while human groans came from the cistern.

Because a steam iron clicks,
a stair board creaks,
a lock barrel shuts safe into position.

Rough

Thieves, and artificial children,
and old men clinging to banisters ...
I recognise them; many's the time
I've looked back on, or forward to,
their choreographies.

"It's supposed to be rough," said
someone's father when I tore my hand
on sandpaper. Now let me say,
if anyone's father tells you that,
there's more than sandpaper on his mind.

And if some thief, or child, mutters
as you pass him in the dripping hall,
or some old guy slouched before a TV set,
the door ajar to his filthy room,
and he red-eyed, barefoot and vested,

says absolutely nothing, stays
mum the way only dads can do,
but peers out from that betrayed beast—
the beached whale of his childhood— then
what he really means to say is
what only that look can explain.

Cinema

Light is the cause of shadow,
children the cause of death.
And when music is heard
silence is never far off.

The actors suffer openly
because they never get to be themselves.

Rivers envy stones, stones rivers.

And while the bird on the hippo's back
seems content enough to wait,
the cinema usherette must wonder
what all these lovers of the dark
are hiding from.

Listening Wind

He crashed the car through the fence,
got out, calmly, picked up the fence,
turned it on its side, then climbed it,

a ladder into sky.
His parents were there before him,
Marie aged 7, Arthur 5.

Still calm, he took their hands.
A man in sandals and a dinner suit
led them through a door

into a wheat field. The words *listening wind*
came to him for a moment—words!—
then they were gone.

He was led to a garden swing
where he knew he was missing something—
his taunted, earth-bound shadow.

And then he awoke, with a start,
horn blowing, wheels spinning
in mud, wheels spinning in his heart.

Chairs

are used to make us sit, not to allow us
to be seated. In this sterile air
who would ever think to disobey
their unvoiced command, their four-square

authority? Just as dumbbells in gyms
test the strength of our devotion
to change, so chairs display our weaknesses:
our need for support, loss of orientation ...

The music of the heart is piped through veins.
Until actors arrive the play can't run.
Snails, though always on the road, like poets
never leave home. And so cannot return.

These are our lived-for insights: but when it comes
nothing brings you down to earth like death,
and the wings of cancer angels tipped
with brown-sugared light like cigarettes ...

And chairs are used to make us sit and think.
Still after still of the history of chairs
will show the unearthly stillness of their existence,
and ours by extension. So, prepare

for wards like these, long shining corridors,
and chairs, not in unassailable rows
but cooling and moving apart like separate planets,
fading into the luxury of shadow.

And though you feel one now against your arse,
nevertheless it is difficult to believe
the chances are you will be in one, like my friend,
when you would slump, but for it, to your knees.

Encounter

Sometimes I like you, but I must confess
most of the time, old man, you wear me down,
slumped there in your chair like a sack
of my father's sacred potatoes back home

in a wintry light. And your so-called news,
that "It is, after all, what they said it would be."
What is? What all? And who said? Is this why
you asked me to come here, to sit and drink tea

and listen to riddles? And anyway who
do you think you are?—looking like the shade
of my own undead father. And when I offer you
a cigarette you don't even respond, instead

you draw yourself up so the light from behind
makes you appear paper-thin, like a leaf
from a Bible. Then, suddenly, finding strength,
just when I think it must be time to leave,

you're all advice: "Don't waste your middle years,"
you say. "Don't treat your life like one big joke."
But when you finally have to pause for breath,
I strike a match, and once again you're smoke.

Passport

Night time especially
in a foreign place, a foreign language,
I feel like a child.

But then it's always night, somewhere,
and more of the world is foreign
than is known, and words, at best,
slip in and out of meaning
like smugglers and stowaways
passing each other on the docks.

So yet another dark and busy night,
a baby sleeping in its mother's arms,
the cars moving slowly onto the ship,
the sea about to take us to ourselves,
to take us home to where the customs officers
will ask if we have anything to declare,
and unless, like Oscar Wilde, we declare our genius,
we may not know who we are standing there
back in the light.

And our passports will offer little help.
We will open them to find kids scowling back,
foreigners who occupy our pasts,
who wear our old clothes and tastes
like uniforms, but refuse to recognise us.
We are all ageing strangers
in their eyes, all under suspicion,
and there is little we can say in our defence.
Some day when we are queuing up at customs,
laden down with Duty Free and bags,
they will barge past without a second glance.

Ghosts

It is we who are the ghosts.
The ones we call ghosts
are frightened of us. After all
we bustle through their homes,
with our ridiculous sense of urgency
scream our obscene love and pain
as if nothing before had ever been important,
or we slump in our own childhoods, watching
age advance from the horizon. Inexorably.

It is we who are the ghosts.
The ones we call ghosts
have nowhere left to hide.
We have chased them out
beyond their precious moon, or down
to the last shadowed lair of earth
where we follow with torches
to scrutinize their drawings, their prayers
made physical, never noticing our own frail scripts
traced in lines of smoke on the trembling air.

Autumn Song

Autumn returns, and again the trees
shed volumes, all of them seeming
to whisper the same word: *sleep.*

It would be very easy now to sleep
and not to wake again, to lie
in the quiet of this city flat

like an old toy or a bloodstain
and let days creep past. It would be
no negation of the light that's been

to accept the dark's embrace and turn
into myself. And yet when I might
give in to this longing, this ancient

weight, I recall how last year,
though the leaves eventually turned to pulp
and rain and snow transformed the street,

then vanished, one day I woke to see
a beam of light from this high window
probe the corners, sweep the room,

a beam I felt myself drawn towards
as a seed must feel itself drawn back
into the world.

Age, Like a Trespasser

Age, like a trespasser, has crept
into your garden, has found
and sat down to your cigarettes,
exhaling the blue smoke of the future.
Look, now he is playing your guitar,
competent and in no hurry,
and now he is simply regarding the sky
as a man might regard his own hands.

Age, like a trespasser, has crept
into your garden, and the apples
fall directly from the trees,
one by one, into his open bag.
Listen, now against his idle whistling
you begin to hear your heart,
and now your dog is barking wildly,
troubled, frightened, by himself.

Age, like a trespasser, has crept
into your garden, and for the first time
you are not alone as the sun goes down,
and familiar colours begin to fade.
Now is the time to confront the darkness
though you cannot see the apple blossoms.
Now you must remain quite calm
though from time to time he calls your name.

Age, like a trespasser, has crept
into your garden, it's night now and you sleep
like cat and mouse, wolf and sheep,
perfect and ancient foes.
But tomorrow, before first light,
enter the garden and gaze at him there,
the crooked spine, those tired old limbs,
then tiptoe back into your woken life.

'In Hell, According to Gary Larson'

In hell, according to Gary Larson,
the maestro will spend eternity
in a room full of gap-toothed yokels,
straw in their hair, banjos on their knees:

And Bach, Shostakovich and Mahler,
and the first song he heard as a boy—
his mother singing Bizet in the kitchen,
shy both in her pain and in her joy—

and his father too the way he hummed those nights
when he had too much to drink, some tune
from his own dead father's lips, the very tune
he ceased to hum the day his fingers died,

the very tune which the night of his own funeral
came for the maestro like a fist of smoke
and dragged him up the chimney into darkness,
away from the attentions of the womenfolk,

beyond the streetlights, up beyond the city,
and down again into some distant room
waiting on the far side of memory
where his father was once again a groom

seated before the piano, and his hands
moved like the hands of a lover,
reaching out, feeling for another,
a New World—all will be forgotten.

For in hell, according to Gary Larson,
the maestro will spend eternity
in a small room full of sweaty yokels:
"Oh! Susanna, don't you cry for me ..."

A Reason for Walking

Words when I think,
thoughts when I word.
Hours with this thought only:
Only words,
not what I feel.

The streets offer
not promise, but escape.
Harmony Row, Misery Hill.
Any named place
better than this.

Back home, the summer sheets
an open book, if blank.
But then the light impression
of our bodies, curled up
in the hieroglyph for love.

Untitled

for Kaja Montgomery

Nothing is mine here
but the symbols of things—
doorways, streetscapes and wings
drawn on the footpath
by a traveller child who,
when the rain washes out his world,
sits up and sings.

How To Be My Heart

Become elastic,
enjoy the solo sound
as well as harmony.
Enjoy the fall—
don't expect ground.
Never move
but never quite be still.
See life as giving
rather than receiving
though the same blood passes
through your grasp like
rosaries, geometries, bound
infinities of love.

Be practical—work.
Keep the orchestra on course,
but imagine the clouds, the skies
you'll never see.
Learn trust. Don't mutiny
when I wade up to my chest in water.
Don't panic if I succumb to drugs
or drink. Don't sink.
Don't ache at every recollection
of a past populated by grief.
Don't succumb to disbelief.
Don't see only darkness up ahead.

Don't stay in bed all day.
Don't lie down and die.
Be there when I need the heart
to tell the unpalatable truth
or the necessary lie.
And give me the sensation of skydiving
when she so much as
walks into my sight.
Make haemoglobin
while the sun shines.
But keep a little oxygen aside.

Between the Lines

Accidental discoveries: coins
Fallen down the backs of easy chairs;
The likeness of a lover, or a friend,
Emerging in a loaf of bread; things
Rising from forgotten places;

And even as you move off towards the future,
Laying what is past, is done, to rest,
Layers of yourself left revealed.

Ignorance is one of the sources of poetry. *

Like a magician who reaches into the hat
On a bad night, his worst in years—
Vera, his assistant, upped and gone,
Even the children noticing his fear—

You find, when you reach into the world,
Occasional if not always blatant signs
Underneath the covers and between the lines.

*Wallace Stevens

Answering Machine

A flashing light will mean I'm not alone.
A moment later maybe I'll hear your voice,
or that of a stranger, or the sound
of someone somewhere having second thoughts

and hanging up. But at least I'll know it means
that someone thinks about me, now and then,
and whoever they prove or do not prove to be,
at least there is a sort of consolation

in the fact that they send a gift of light,
a sign to welcome me on my return.
You are not alone, it will say, first thing,
the green light of the answering machine.

Or else: *how desperate you've become
for love, the glimmer of surprise,
alone there in the doorway of your room
like a man before an endless, starless sky.*

Murder

Drumlin country. Passing through
on the Derry bus, it's not so strange—
the scattered towns, the same small houses,
the same sky both sides of the border—
except for the sudden apparition
on a bend in the road of a squad of men
in uniforms, and more in the ditch,
scanning the hills for signs of movement,
or staring down their gun barrels
into infinity. And then something else
wrapped in black there by the roadside,
a thing you tell yourself must be hay
baled in plastic and probably lost
when a trailer took this turn too fast
as the bus is waved on and you look up
at the collective noun for a gathering of crows.

Way of Peace

i.m. Eamon Keating

In Adidas sneakers
and white karate suit
with the simple crest—

a dove round a fist,
Wado Ryu,
the way of peace—

down the Downs,
past the gate house gate,
a chubby druid,

a breathing oak,
a shifting mountain,
following patterns

modelled on monkeys,
eagles and cranes,
stray dogs and dragons,

bird man of Portlaoise,
puff-jowled adder,
dancing bear,

a man in his 60s
somehow still
sane enough to play;

and me, 16,
hidden among trees,
glimpsing the way.

The Dead Man's Clothes

The dead man's clothes
were willed to the village orphans
so that, those long summer evenings,
he was everywhere,
moving through the fields
until the sun went down,
bloodily.

The villagers loved it, calling
Gretel, Hansel, Romulus,
and watching the old man's shoulder turn
or the big baggy arse
that was his alone come
to a sudden, billowing halt.

Except his wife. Unable
to decide whether this was flattery
or insult, she kept herself
to herself, shut up inside,

while the village orphans
came in from the fields, their hands
reddened from picking berries
and trailing mothballs in the street
like puffs of light.

from *As the Hand, the Glove* (2001)

Milkmen

The doorbell rings. I go.
I'm fourteen. That's how it is,
no need to stop or think.

It's the milkman's eldest son,
putting a brave face on it,
wearing his father's shade.

So quietly he pours the milk,
pours its at-first almost thin,
then rolled, then muddy sound

until the gallon is filled.
I close the door and wait
for the milk to settle down.

Years later—for it is years
already—I begin to know,
what it means, this opening

of doors, of silences, to accept
things not made on the spot
but handed over: love, inheritance.

Eden

Sundays were where flowers blazed
in water. The sky bled
and organ music cooled like bread
in the stony light. In a kind of daze

that seemed to last forever, I went
to our two-tree orchard to catch fruit
in my open shirt, holding my breath
so I might hear the creak of the nuts

and bolts that held the world in place
and would release it. And if it was
winter or spring, if frost had put lace
finishing on the hedgerows, or if tiny paws

of new growth were pushing up through earth,
I'd take all that in too
in that between-time place where one thing at least was true:
they *were* blood relations, death and birth.

No Man's Land

The world began with our house.
At night if you listened hard
you could hear a whole universe
still forming. Out in the back yard

where the Milky Way stretched between
the roofs of cut-stone sheds,
bats flittered in the beams
of our flashlights, their tiny heads

like turned-out pockets. Closer,
water dripped or gushed, the dog
sensed something, cocked an ear
then stood as if the hands of a clock

had frozen somewhere. I was back
in No Man's Land again, a place
I loved, and feared: the black,
damp air pressed against my face

like a hand. Behind me at the door
separating inside and out,
womb and world, a dozen or more
slugs would gather, dumb, devout

as guard dogs, thick as eels
or old rope, drawn by the light
or warmth of the house, the wheels
and spirals of their journeys bright

as silver dust in honey. So when
the time came to go back, to leave
that strange land, head down I ran
as fast as I could, leaping clear

of the lair of teeming serpents, and with luck
making it across the threshold
into human light again, awe-struck
by strangeness, bringing strangeness home.

Hall of Mirrors

"I'd like ..." says the stranger standing before me, "that!"
He points to something over my shoulder and waits.
It's a Travel Agency, though my father calls it The Shop,
and brochures that glisten with pictures of girls in all states

of undress, stretched on white sands or by pools,
cover the walls and counters behind me. I know
without looking round. But when I reluctantly do
(awkward teenage), it's something I've not seen before:

he's pointing to a small gold mirror containing
a fish-eye microcosm of the room we're in.
It's like the room in Van Eyck's *Arnolfini Wedding*
except, of course, I'm in V-neck and flares, and, thin

as a rake though I am, sport a Bruce Lee medallion.
It's important to face the world with an iron will.
So, to this strangely familiar stranger's reflection
I say, "Sorry, but that mirror is not for sale."

But before I can explain this is a Travel Agency,
a place you go when you want to go some place,
and not some newsagent's or hall of mirrors,
my father comes out and says, "Good man, you're there."

And in an instant it's just the two of us alone.
The stranger has vanished, as in Abracadabra.
It's the 1970s still, and all I know
begins with Abbey Road and ends with Abba.

Tracks

Now my dog is dead,
paw prints in the concrete path
follow me instead.

Potion

Summer. My mother's time. A place
anything was possible — staying up
late into the evening, swapping grace
after meals for ice cream and a cup,

never a glass, of that special juice
she made from sugar, a few lemons and
some kind of powder whose arcane use
could not have been restricted to our clan

though no one I've asked among my friends
remembers their mothers in that queue
in Hipwell's chemists where mine would spend
half of every Saturday, saying "And how are you?"

to every new arrival. Which is strange.
For she added it to water and made water change.

Doors and Windows

My father sold them, doors and windows,
entrances, exits, idyllic views
from houses not constructed yet
though mapped out with such absolute

precision that those wooden frames
we'd spend evenings stacking to the sky,
then half days driving and unloading
in windswept fields, before our eyes

transformed. Fingers smarting
from the rasp of wood, I'd press
a fist into a palm, count to ten
and watch my breath trace silent protest

in the air, then count to ten again
while he, as I now know, in his own way—
saliva in his palm—secured the deal
and made a friend he hoped would someday pay,

though many never did ... Then we were off,
the builders stood there, watching through the glass
that wasn't even in those windows yet, and overhead
the Milky Way already settling into place.

The Scarecrow

was Hannigan's (Hannigan being
the one who had the brother
who went to the dance and never
came home again), standing there
west of the high thicket of briars,
arms outstretched, no hands,
a bag of air for a head, pants
the brother left behind him in his wake,
the brother they never mentioned afterwards
for peace' sake ...

Easy to get lost
in the endless ravelling of thoughts
that ran between all things, back then.
But back then we went, and went again,
to that top field to stare
into the absence of his face:
Hannigan's scarecrow,
in that NorthSouthEastWest
world of things half known,
an open secret.

Neighbours

They were the ones we told jokes about,
the red-necked, spud-thick family up the road:
how she smashed the car into the gate
going for her driving test, how once the door
came away in the father's hand like a sheet

of old wallpaper. And then their kid.
Helping daddy one day paint the fence
around their concrete garden, he knocked the tin
then ran away in tears, his yellow footprints
and their yellow footprints all over the street

like a dance-step map. Wee Johnny,
which is what they called him, never seemed
quite right after that. The poor wee mon, he
was frightened of his shadow. At Hallowe'en,
kids knocked on their door and threw him money

to see if he'd cry. Which he always did.
In school they ganged up on him in the yard
and made him sing *The Sash*. More than once he peed
his pants. More than once his furious dad
had to come and take him home at speed.

When the sister married, true to form
the old man drank so much he fell face first
into the wedding cake. The honeymoon,
in Ballyshannon, was a total farce.
The groom met an old flame and he was gone.

Their flat-faced dog liked to chase parked cars.
The mother opened doors in her dressing gown.
We laughed till we were sick, and then we laughed
even more. The day before they finally left town
the kid came second in a boxing match.

Supermarket

Fifteen, out of the altar boys
on the grounds of age, and height, I found
my first part-time employment in
the only supermarket in town,

eating chocolate, sweeping floors,
spotting young ones, talking soccer
and always keeping the oldest
meat to the front.

On days when only one or two
roamed the aisles, it fell to me
to turn the music way down slow,
so Mrs X would waltz and dream

her way past towers of toilet rolls,
would stand and stare at cans of beans
or dickied-up photos of some Fido
selling cat in chunks.

And when the place was stuffed, was packed
with dripping shoppers, little brats,
their hands like magnets, and the girls
in pencil skirts from the nearby banks,

I'd whip the tape out, that big 8-track
Strauss-filled sandwich, and lift the place
into the 20th century, volume up
as high as it went,

so that Mrs X was sent skating past
Mrs Y, and their men became
trolley Jackie Stewarts, each aisle
a freeway, the whole shop a maze,

a wonder, like the streets of a town
in a film that has been speeded up
so that all the citizens go tearing around
like so many ants.

But there was no film, only me
watching from the top of the office stairs
as the roll of flimsy paper crept
ever upwards in the cash register

manned by a girl in a navy smock,
stenographer of all desires
and needs in that dreary,
dreaming midland town.

And I wondered often how she felt,
the most powerful person in that world
of haughty managers, sweet-talking reps
and foul-mouthed butchers, their hands and skirts

covered in maps of blood, when,
as if someone somewhere had pulled the plug
or broken the spell, the roll spun out, spun free,
and that dream was gone.

Flesh

The spirit, despite bad press,
loves the flesh.

It enjoys nothing more
than body odour,

the warmth of a crotch
or the electric touch

of lips. Those dark religions
which have banned the nether regions

to the netherworld, to hell,
can cast all the spells

they like, can single out for blame
those who refuse to feel shame

about their bodies—children, the old,
the 'savage' inhabitants of the Third World,

but most of all those women of loose morals
whose torture is somehow part of the quarrel

about sanctity and sin
and the vessels the soul is to be found in.

Enough idols and bones!
Enough gleaming chalices and altar stones!

I say it again: the spirit loves
the flesh, as the hand the glove.

And if you doubt me, ask my dying father
which he would rather:

to be done at last with love and pain,
or to leave, but then come back to flesh again.

Am

i.m. Nicholas Boran

1.35 a.m.
I look at my watch and see
my life story:
I thirty-five am.

And if I press this button here
I get the date, 1999,
the year when my *am* begins to mean
something new, something else,
your *was*, your *is no longer*,
the year of your death.

The Disappearing Act

These hands take things,
shake things, make things
disappear.

These hands, literally,
for hands are all there are
in this dark space

lit up with hope and purpose,
sharp as bright ideas
against emptiness.

One, the left,
makes the 'watch this' sign
then points to the right

and plucks a perfect flower
out of thin air
thick now with applause.

The kids go wild.
For them, this breaking of the cause
and effect chain

is a kind of dream
with evidence. Already you can see
their tiny hands repeat

the stylised moves.
Though doubts remain.
As the curtain falls

into the magician's
battered case, the birthday child's
upset, confused:

"Ma," she wails,
"make him do it again."
But, as Ma well knows,

there's no going back.
Life's unfair? Well, tough.
She smiles at friends,

the other single parents,
and then leans in
towards her own little gem:

"Magic's not like fighting, love,"
I imagine her say. "It's over,
not beginning, when the gloves come off."

Haiku

Lovers in the park,
her hands holding his hands down:
gift of powerlessness.

Chaos

*Simple shapes are inhuman. They fail to resonate
with the way nature organises itself or with the way
human perception sees the world.*
—James Gleick

By the time I get there, the house is just a shell.
On one wall I see the marks where my father's keys
hung above the range, and opposite
a door that once led somewhere. Little else.

The kitchen has become the yard once more.
So much for expansion. And the hall,
once set with in-laid tiles, is now a sprawl
of stones and mortar. The front door

has to be propped up to hold the street
at bay. And overhead, without beams,
floors or walls, upstairs is one big room
filled with unfamiliar light.

Months from now, my father dead, we'll be back,
my mother, sisters, brothers and myself,
to visit a new two-storey space
with its bland smoothness, its almost perfect lack

of character. In its one big window
we'll line up side by side to face the street,
and have our pictures taken from the path
outside, cast as the resident ghosts.

For the moment, surrounded by the mess
of rubble, the flotsam and jetsam of childhood,
it doesn't feel as bad as I thought it would.
But then the worst loss is the slowly dawning loss.

For S with AIDS

When a star dies, my love, my man,
when it gets so tired, burnt out, so heavy,
it starts to fall back into itself,
it starts to grow in density, shrink
until, at last, there comes a time
when light escapes from it no more,
when time means nothing any more,
when science, naming and love itself
wring their hands at the hospital door.
Nothingness, absence, passing, loss ...
our secret, sleeping partners, S.

2.

Ouroboros, the mythological serpent
consuming itself, renewing itself,
the snake of Eden, snake of the tree,
the serpent coiled round the staff of being
still found on local chemists' signs,
like the one where you binged on vitamins—
what was it, three years back?—all set
to fight what you were sure was 'flu,
then toothache, backache, headache, gout ...
Now your name cannot be spoken here
in these half-lit corridors leading nowhere
but I can hear your playful hiss,
snake brother, snake lover, S.

3.

Close up, the red-shift of apple skin
is a microcosm of the universe,
at once unbounded and finite.
See, what they did not tell us, S,
was that in Eden there were many trees
and many apples on their boughs,
on the skin of each whole galaxies,
in the core a constellation of seeds.
Unpicked the apple would still have fallen
to return to death and be born again
in whole new trees, in each apple of which
new seeds, new orchards, whole new Edens.

PS—And S, the snake's sloughed skin
is what he was, or will be, not what he is.

Afterlife

i.m. Lar Cassidy

They're back in the back yard at it,
at it strong,
in that creaking red Escort
with the headlights left on

so they flood the room.
I've only just heard
about your death over the phone,
those few and terrible words

which the living must accept
as a new place to begin,
and I was about to do what
I've done before, fling

something, lift the window
and fling something to bring
those shaggers to their senses—
Do it all you like, sing

if you're so moved
but kill the lights. There are souls
trying to sleep (or mourn or brood)
under your jerking strobes ...

On other nights, and, yes,
there have been months on end
since I set in here like stressed
concrete, the only godsend

the heat in these woollen folds,
on those nights
before I knew you, long before
we even met, when quiet

was the last thing I needed,
I might have got up, opened
this window to roar my delirium
or, more likely, left unspoken

the extent of my irritation
and just stood there or lain
here as I do now in the nation
of one we all become again

when the lights go out.
The time of listening.
But tonight you're dead, though not yet
out of reach—if anything

all the great teachings teach
is true—so maybe it's right
that in the light of all their fuss
out there and the darkness of my wait

in here for the day's return,
you should be rising up
on this twin helix, carried aloft
or on to where our wavering hope

in an afterlife,
in a better life and love
and place than this,
will be, if there is a god, absolved.

169

Grief

There is no consolation.
The streets of the city
are windswept, forsaken.
Broken glass
glistens on the footpath.
The train station
you've come to know so well
is deserted. Newspapers
litter the tracks, worthless
as memories. A bag
with nothing in it but a rat,
the only sign of life.

You hear
the lonely echo of your footsteps
unable to find you,
see your shadow
wind around you,
dissolve into you then
reappear behind you as the lights
along the platforms pick you out
one by one by one, like rooms
or bright ideas you wander through
but do not recognise
the meaning of.

It's night. Keep
your eyes open. If you weaken
it will all be over, you'll have learned
nothing from the nightmare
yet again. If you tire or start

to drift, splash
your face with water, stand
by the keening hand-dryer
all night long if that is what it takes,
in that bruising light
in which the junkie
cannot hope to find the vein.

Unbuild

I think the stairs bare.
I recall the tacks,
all three boxes we whacked
into them back there,

back then in the past, now
all for one and one for all
drawn out, withdrawn, or
the right word—recalled.

Then the stairs itself.
From the corridor of space
I remove the zigzag shelf
down which I raced,

up which I crawled
when they sent me off to bed.
And now when night falls
I go back again,

I unbuild the house.
Stone by blessed stone
I have taken it apart,
and still it is not gone.

Merrion House Sestina

I live and work on the top floor at the back
of this four-storey building. Mostly I go
through the motions. Each morning as I watch
a gradual transformation take place
in these lanes and car-parks, the light
returning to a city that seemed lost

only hours before, it's the lost
I feel drawn to, those neighbours in the back
of my mind in a house where even daylight
no longer enters. While office workers go
about their business, resuming their places
behind drawn blinds and screens, I watch

for things I can't explain to them: that swatch
of tarmac, now matt, now glossed
with a shower of rain; the commonplace
miracle of buddleia; and here, back
from her travels above the archipelago
of rooftops, that female gull, in flight

a creature without weight until she alights
with a thud in the nest above me to watch
over her young. And though it's not so long ago
since other families grew up here, felt lost
as they waited for a parent to come back
with food, or news, with proof of other places

beyond this house, that was another place,
another time. These days there's just my light-
sleeping beloved, myself, and gulls. And at the back
of this maze of lanes, late at night, the watching,
cautious eyes of an urban fox. Have the last
secretaries suffering from the vertigo

of computer screens noticed her? I've seen her go
down these lanes, a shadow in a place
of shadows, a creature that has lost
one world and claimed another. Before the light
returns, she slips into the spaces no one watches,
no one remembers. And then I'm here, back

in the go-slow chair of poetry, the resident hunchback
of this haunted, haunting house where my wristwatch
like myself struggles out of loss and into light.

Literature

His penis hanging between his legs
like a vandalised telephone, or some
deep-sea creature that cannot bear
solitude, so it hangs on,

this naked man is what I am—
and yet how unlike me he seems,
surprised in this mirror I was dashing past
on my way through the house at 4 a.m.

And when a light comes on somewhere,
quick as a flash he turns away
like a man who would keep his truth concealed,
this Rosebud, this Jekyll, this Dorian Gray.

The Wheel

for Theo Dorgan

I found a wheel.
That is my sorrow.
It cannot sit still
and be itself.
It wants to lift, shift, roll things, be
the centre of change.

I give it change.
I take it to the theatre;
it squeaks.
I play it the most wonderful
classical music;
it lies there and groans.
I give it drink,
an obvious mistake;
it loses its former
good humour, roars
like a bull with a lance in its throat,
totals the room.

Then this afternoon,
coming home
from a match (where it leaned
like a headstone),
what did we pass?
The car plant:
cogs, rivets, those white conveyor belt
wheels by the score, wheels
like a line of gleaming Os,

in continuous surprise.
And, no surprise, the wheel
went into a spin, a whirr, a positive—
Yeats's word—gyre!
It took me everything I had
to get us both back home
and settled down. And now,

it's late. Now I'm tired.
The grate has given up
the last memory of heat.
Sheets of icy rain are drawing in
from the North-West, the North-East,
and it's clear
why the Romans took one look at us out here
in Winterland
and said, no way.

The kind of night
when there's nothing better
than the promise of rest, of sleep,
of Hibernation Once Again
as they used to say;

when all I want
is just to sit like this
and listen to the sound of nothing much,

there's the wheel, the wheel
cries like a child for my touch.

Wireless

Was there anyone back then who didn't love
its name—the only thing on earth defined
by absence? Wire-less. That household god
looking down on us all, a coffin of sorts
until someone switched it on

and it hummed into life, hummed
even between stations the song
of origin, of background radiation.

And how it lit up
slowly then glowed like the ghost
of a hurt, like the ghost of my father
on a chair, reaching for its dial,
a safecracker breaking into the vaults
of sound, or breaking out into the world beyond
our sleepy, listening midland town
in a house since vanished.

2.

Here in the park, more than thirty years on,
a group of men sit and listen
to a football match. The neat beds and borders
might be the sun-dappled vines
of Marconi's own vineyard, so great

is their passion, their excitement and my own
sense of loss. To close my eyes now is to run
back through those vines, down our yard,

back past the must-smelling sheds, is to find
my father still there in the dark on that chair

staring into deep space, as if
he had known all along I'd be back,
that the message he had sent, like a voice
down invisible lines, would unite us again.

First Lesson in Alchemy

Rabbit, swan, deer, butterfly ...
Out of nowhere, and with empty hands,
my father brought the shadow world to life.

Usually it happened late at night:
he'd light a candle, fix it on the stand,
then rabbits, swans, deer, that butterfly

and creatures I had never heard described
changed one into the other. Understand?
My father brought the shadow world to life.

Spelled out like this, it doesn't seem quite right,
quite true, this miracle of the midlands
where rabbits, swans, deer or even butterflies

were seldom to be seen in broad daylight
in the few square miles that confined our lives back then.
My father brought a shadow world to life?

And yet that's what he did. Before our eyes
his simple gesture made the known expand.
Rabbits, swans, deer, butterflies ...
Now my father gives the shadow world new life.

Machines

One night in York Street
almost ten years back—so much
drink and junk around the place

it was hard to say
just who was us, or them—one night
as I lay down to sleep on my own

cold slab of light, it started up:
below in the street, a car alarm
wielding its terrible, surgical blade

of sound. Across the way,
the College of Surgeons grinned in the night
like a skull, like a stack of skulls,

but it was hard not to cheer
when someone from a few doors up
suddenly appeared. A yard brush

like a weapon in his hands, he climbed
onto the gleaming bonnet where he stood
and began to swing,

first with aim and intent, so that
one by one the front lights went in, then
the indicators, windscreen wipers, the windscreen itself ...

and then like some half-man, half-thing
swung, swung, swung, swung,
swung till his muscles must have ached,

till the mangled brush tumbled from his grip
and he stopped, turned, looked up at us and roared
as if his spirit could no longer be contained

by the silence, by the darkness,

by the slow-motion tragedy of
so much of Dublin back in those
and still in these dehumanising days.

Housework

All day I have been squeezing shirts
as if they were necks. In a kind
of blind fury, I like to take it out
on things that need washing, shifting or,
if I'm lucky, smashing up. There is
perfection in a filthy bag of coal
standing in a street as cars speed past,
and something more than gravity fights back
every step of four steep flights of stairs.
And who could deny there's something just as good
as the blood of enemies or the sweat of love
in coal-dust handprints on your shirt
and a bag that might contain a corpse
inside the door? It's almost May
and not even cold, but damn it feels
better now already. It is worth
two whole days of blisters out of seven
to see the furniture rearranged, remade,
piles of papers banished, strange space
making itself at home, as something else
finds itself at ease and settles in,
something that is without, as yet, a name,
and outside at least one man's laundry waves
its flag of surrender in the breeze.

The Washing of Feet

It's the simplest form of healing:
late at night,
the washing of feet.

When the light called sky
is an absence,
when the traffic's asleep;

when song
is a physical thing
needing physical shape

but you're just so worn out
facing darkness again
and those brave

tulips and roses
in Merrion Square
have long since turned in

to the dark, cottony
breath that simmers
inside of them.

When the world
is a cave, a dungeon,
when the angels retreat,

return to this tiny
pacific ocean,
to the washing of feet.

Turning

i.m. Michael Hartnett

The desk calendar on its last leaves.
In the lampshade a tiny spider weaves
a winter shroud.
The sky is a single cloud
darker still to the west.
The skull of a martin's nest
grins in the eaves.

A Box of Keys

A box the size of a small suitcase.
It was the buildings he'd misplaced.

Tears

I like to cry
I like to cry so much
first thing I did when I was born
was cry
cry up a storm,
cry up
two small torrents
two strong currents.
The world
slapped me as a signal
to begin
so I began
as I determined to continue
with tears.

All through my childhood years
I cried, sometimes
howling my release
my relief
my glad return
to the vale of tears.
Right up until the time
the hormones came
out of hiding
out of waiting
and began
their slow tour of my body
tears
came easily.

In my teens they stopped.
My tears went underground
like the small stream
I'd played in as a boy
before the town grew up.
I knew they were there.
I felt their pull,
their attraction, but found
neither spring nor river mouth
where they might whisper
back to the greater
rhythm of ocean,
the ocean of tears.

No tears for instance
at seventeen
where there was more
to cry about
than I could explain,
and far too few
in recent years
when the brightest light
in the night sky
began to fade.

But now
I'm always close to tears,
at home with tears,
and not only my own but yours,
my love. I see or hear
or somehow sense
that hot swell as I cross a room
and pass a stranger in the street

as if all eyes
were forcing me to recognise
something in the air.

And I have seen myself
in the future, prepared
to move on, move out
of the way, the room,
through doors maybe
but back to a place
where tears are rolling
down my face
as the world lifts
its hands from my flesh
and I am lighter, light again,
and the sound of that
original slap
runs backwards before
all is still again,
all is quiet again
and my eyes sit still
in my skull again
only salt now, dry salt now
where once there were,
I'm glad to say,
my tears.

Still Life with Carrots

When I discover a carrot, like this one,
grown old, forgotten on a shelf
behind bottles of oil, herbs and spices,
all those *nouveaux arrivés*, I feel myself

drawn to it. It's as if all
the wonderful meals my life has been made of,
the exotic tables at which I have sat
had never existed, as if during love-

making a former lover had come
into my mind, or a neighbour, long dead
had knocked on the door and let himself in,
as of old, trailing the earth from his grave.

The politeness accosts me. Almost as frail
as my father in his hospital bed
those last long months, this carrot seems
to have something to tell me. The fact is, in the end,

the formidable weakens, the once proud
become stooped and sad. The lost
no longer recognise themselves.
And so it goes for all our vegetable loves:

the pea dries up; the tomato weeps
and weeps an ectoplasmic mess;
lettuce browns like an old book;
potatoes send up flares of distress;

but carrots just age there, waiting to be found,
as the plates on the table, like the planets, go around.

Falun Gong

The young Chinese men and women
barely move at all. That's what's so strange.
You've read that back in China they are outlawed,
hunted down like terrorists. Arraigned,
convicted and sentenced for crimes
against the state, many are not seen again.
And now today you take a short-cut through the park
and here they are, a small man dressed in silk
and an even smaller girl in a yellow tracksuit,
breaking all known laws: they are standing still
in the middle of rush-hour, for all the world
like two figures from a painting by Chagall,
the moment before flight, their arms outstretched,
reaching towards the limits of themselves.

Filling Station

after a painting by Edward Hopper

The man in the filling station looks like death.
I say, "Must get some quiet days around here."
He doesn't even answer. Instead
he turns his back, his polyester shirt sleeves
whipping around his skinny tattooed arms.

I see him with many lovers in his past
in that big crumbling cinema over the road,
a tough guy then, a man fathers might watch
if he didn't move so fast, if he didn't know,
or seem to, that the boys from those small farms

back up the way were out to get him, that
given half a chance they'd stamp him out
like a cigarette dropped in a barn.
There was fire there once, of that no doubt.
Now he looks as if he's made of ash,

as if the wind could break him, or the rain
coming in a black cloud from the north
might wash him clean away, leaving not a trace,
unless, maybe, a single postcard worn
to shreds in a back pocket. *Baby, I can't wait ...*

The Raising of Lazarus

after a painting by Aelbert Ouwater

The kitchen was a bombsite
the night my father found the corpse
of our neighbour Paddy Walsh
spread across the floor like
a misfired human cannonball.

He called the Guards. The priest arrived
and told him to take a stroll across
to Lewis's pub. A double short
seemed wiser than his usual pint
after that terrible shock.

An hour later, the pub full
of red-eyed mourners, who limped in
but Paddy Walsh, the man himself,
not looking bad for having gone
all week without a square meal.

The Watchers

after a photograph by Ernst Haas

More than ever I wonder about them,
the unknown people who sit watching us
in small rooms somewhere, surrounded by
over-flowing ashtrays, plastic cups

and walls of screens. What their names are;
their ages and sexes; what they think
when they think they're not thinking; what they see
today that they could not have seen

their first day on the job. How must it feel
to hover all day like a minor god
or angel, unable to make
the slightest difference? Unless they love

being the watchers, unless what they need
is the distance, the comfort of fiction,
it must be hell. The hours and days
must drag by in those hot-air balloons,

those diving bells. I imagine marks
on walls counting off the first kiss,
then the hundred-thousandth kiss, and suppose
zooming in and out must loose its charm.

And when the shift is over, when the next
wave of angels arrives, what do they feel
as they step out into these same streets to become
just another random group of subjects to the pals

who will wach them now? These men
and women suddenly made flesh
and blood, hands inside gloves
and scarves wrapped around their necks

against the cold like the bandages
that give the invisible man his shape.
How could they not look back up into the lens
and mouth the words: *I know you're there.*

The Voice on the Jukebox Sang 'Maybe ...'

In a black hat and black coat,
with the kind of movements a crow makes
when it tries to tear itself away
wing by wing from hot tar,
he was there in the bar.

What happened next? Well, no one spoke
for a start; no one, I suppose,
had any words they felt might match
the 3-dimensional shock of him,
this tongue of black fire—man,

the only animal with foreknowledge
of his own imminent death.
All right, come on, joke's over,
said the barmaid in mid forward
bend that might have flashed a breast

to some old drunk ... But Christ, not this,
a man stood there, held there, run through
with the current of his heart, unhid
in this one moment she would deny
that at once denies her and demands she live.

A Natural History of Armed Conflict

The wood of the yew
made the bow. And the arrow.
And the grave-side shade.

The Melting Pot

Sick in New York, in Chinatown,
I go to a Ukranian doc
who gives me a shot in the arm and says
"Straight to bed for you, my friend." So I book

into the nearest run-down hotel,
no curtains in the windows, stains
like maps on the mattress, a hanger stuck
in the top of the TV, half cross, half weathervane.

For the first few hours I think I'm going to die.
Bathed in sweat, I lie on my back
flicking between grainy newsreels, kung-fu
soap operas and some kind of chat

show where everyone is shouting all the time.
And then I dream, neither awake nor asleep:
a tiny Chinese man is calling out my name
from the bottom of a stairs, and up

where I am stretched out, a kid whose hands
are covered in food, in blood, leans over me until
his face is a mirror to mine, and smiles.
"Island?" he says. "Never heard of it."

Transportation

The starched white sheets billowed in the wind.
It was like being on a galleon,
a hundred miles, a thousand years from shore,
hauling the line at my mother's command, setting

a course for home.

Penknife

Still smelling of oranges
after years in this drawer
among buttons, paperclips,
envelopes, old specs ...

a present from you;
designed to sever,
it's the one thing
that somehow connects.

Lost and Found

Sometimes now I see my father
up in Heaven, wandering around
that strange place where he gathers up
what other souls no longer want,
as all his life he gathered
unloved things.

As if on a screen I see
his big frame bend, his bony hands
reach down for a rusted pin,
a nail, a coin from some lost kingdom.
One day it will be the very thing
someone will need.

And when the tears become too much
and this damned bed might be a field,
I sit up wondering how the hell
the world can always find more fools
to lose things and be lost themselves
and carry on.

Then something in my heart gives in,
and I know, as if I'd always known
deep down, that all that trash, that old
Christmas wrapping, those balls of string,
the belts, belt buckles, the left-hand gloves,
the dozens of pair of worn-out shoes
and toeless socks, the blown light bulbs,
the coils of wire and threadbare screws,
the broken clocks, the plastic bags

folded neatly, the leaking pens
and dried-up markers, the ink-stained rags
and blotting paper, the bashed-in tins
of washers, plasters, needles and lint
were never his at all, were meant
for me.

Hand Signals

A winter's evening. Cycling through the rain,
fingers clenched around the handgrips,
I'm remembering those nights my hands could pass
for log rafts or the fighter planes
that dive-bombed the water in the bath,
or in shadow play could shape-shift
into rabbits, swans, deer ... But times change.

People change. Determined to make them hard,
in my early teens I filled a bag with sand
and bullied it for hours. Behind the wall
of the Shaolin temple that was our back yard
I prepared for battle. Learning to fall
and rise from the dead, I'd pretend
to be first the assassin, then the bodyguard.

My hands were weapons. When they chopped air,
the air whistled. Against invisible foes
they whirled like knives. Half-inch deal
might as well have been paper: I could bear
the pain by not thinking about it. Still
my long fingers have always looked like those
strangely moon-faced figures there

steering the way. And when I stop at the lights
to flex and warm them, I hear the bones creak
and grate in my flesh. I see how my blood
after all has deserted them. So tonight,
mission accomplished, storm withstood,
I'll start over, take in reverse these streets
back to our house, our bedroom, where I'll find

you stretched out in sleep, as singular
as any unknown world. I'll rest one hand
on your warm forehead and dream once more
of a home from home, a place where all hands are
like the Famous Five, tired after adventure,
camped out in their zipped-up sleeping bags,
side by side, and gazing up at stars.

Driving into History

Once in a while, morning sunshine
filtered through the peeling paint and rust
of that old black banger, perched
like a stylite up on concrete blocks

in our back garden. The seats were torn,
the wooden dashboard was an altar to insect death,
and yet my first boyhood trips into the world
were in that wheel-less, if not quite lifeless wreck.

But since they took the garden to build a bypass
to our once congested, now double-bypassed town,
I dream little of either speed or novelty
and, truth to tell, I scarcely know the names

of all these cars out here. Now all I wish

is time enough for them to age and rust,
to end up up on blocks in some child's life,
twentieth century coins down behind their seats,
their vacant windscreens open to the light.

The Engine

With a four-sided aluminium key
and one hand clamped around the wheels
to hold them still, I hold my breath
and wind the engine of the small grey train.

I am five or six years old and I wind
for the soft creaking of the spring,
for the pull of these four small wheels
like the heart-throb of some living thing.

Later when I carve my name in wood
or later again stub out cigarettes
it will be with this same motion, but for now
I wind to be here, beside myself,

and with the last possible, last permissible turn
to release the perfect single ping
then watch as the engine heads out with the news,
a thing beyond me, a thing singing.

New Poems

A Man is Only as Good ...

A man is only as good
as what he says to a dog
when he has to get up out of bed
in the middle of a wintry night
because some damned dog has been barking;

and he goes and opens the door
in his vest and boxer shorts
and there on the pock-marked wasteground
called a playing field out front
he finds the mutt with one paw

raised in expectation
and an expression that says Thank God
for a minute there I thought
there was no one awake but me
in this goddamned town.

Fetch

Again and again she comes back to me
to place it by my feet, today's
old piece of flotsam or bonfire debris
dug out from the heap and blessed
with a kind of magic.

Dog-given, the least of things
may be treasure for a day.

And how she spends these days,
this love-struck mutt,
stretched out along a neighbour's wall,
comically shadowing the postman,
or, despite the wind and ice-flecked rain
that keeps every other dog indoors,
bounding out across this desolate park
as if it were a summer's meadow, alive
to the possibility of play.

Hours, I imagine, she has spent already
running like this between her home
and mine, her world and ours,

to bring me a stick,
to chase that stick, to seize that stick
and then come back with that stick so tight
between her jaws it sometimes seems
she will never release it, that she has changed
the rules and very purpose of the game,

and had I the strength
I might lift her clear
or she might lift me clear
of this rain-locked planet.

The Magic Roundabout

There was always something on his mind,
that Dougal. Such a curious dog,
his head like the head of little Florence
invariably cocked to one side or the other ...

Each week something lost would have to be found.
Mystery would descend like a fog
on their simple, predictable world, but Dougal's innocence
if not stupidity would visit even more bother

on his friends, in truth strange folk themselves, inclined
to going round in circles, to monologue
and soliloquy, but showing complete indifference
to the voice that came from the sky. Plodder

that Dougal was, evidently blind
to the hallucinatory smog
the others passed their time in (hardly a fence
in all that countryside and, even odder,

mushrooms throughout the year, outlined
against the backdrop greens and greys); and slog
that adding two and two became, or telling the difference
between night and day, a rock and some small creature,

rather than take a break to let the plot unwind
in all its perfect nonsense, all its bog
logic or woodland magic, with the impotence
of a hero he'd persevere ever further

after a meaning he could never hope to find.
Not in a world like this. He should have played a log,
stretched out and waited for Zebedee's late appearance,
his "It's time for tea." The poor old tutter,

to use my family's word for a fool, could he not just find
a nice soft spot to lie back on and, like the mere cog
in the machine he was, seize the chance
to glimpse, even once, the hands of god the father?

Nature's Gentleman

Are these the same flowers, old friend,
the wild flowers we stopped to admire
only weeks ago, their yellows and reds
ablaze in the field to the back of your house?
This morning I imagine your neighbours' kids out
filling their arms with them.

And was that your coffin we saw last year
exploring these woods, an ancient oak
that leaned out precariously over the path
where you walked every day of your life,
granting you one last season of shade,
adding one final ring to its grain.

Jupiter

It was the year I first saw Jupiter,
just an arm's length away down a telescope
someone had swiped from his brother's room
and hid in his coat. From a crater

in the old sandpit, the interference
of the sodium-yellow lights of the town
was wiped clean, wiped clear, the universe
no longer just a cloud of chalk dust

against the blackboard of sky. And there above us,
if trembling, coming in and out of focus,
Jupiter itself, the famous Red Spot
the only thing we talked about for weeks.

Until that night when the first young fellow
in Leaving Cert year—and, Christ, only now
do I see how well it was named for him,
for them—made his way out there alone,

his duffel coat over his arm concealing
what should have been someone's brother's telescope.

Tent

Maurice has lost his virginity
in a tent, or so he claims, out beyond
the new hotel with a foreign girl
who happened to be hitching through.

When the jeering has at last died down,
most of us grin, kick at the earth
or stare into the middle distance, shy
of being the first to give himself away.

That evening, like tourists on a trail
to some historic battleground, we troop
all the way out, the full mile or more
to the now famous field where the girl is

long since gone, though yes there does appear
to be a faint impression in the grass:
rectangular, for all the world like a door
and big enough for a man to pass through.

Bees

It was the summer of bees.
Everywhere we went,
up to the coffee shop
or down to the beach for a swim,
one of us ended up
up on his feet, on her feet,
making violent, impotent gestures
in the humid air.

Bees were everywhere.
Kids at the sweetshop
in short sleeves, half in despair,
held ice creams at arm's length
and struggled against tears.
In the local post office
the usually blank-faced teen
stood three feet back from the glass
cowering in fear.

People bought papers,
rolled them up and wielded them
like bats. The neighbour's dog
seemed almost on the verge
of a heart attack
but still carried on
trying to intercept their ceaseless
warp and weave.

But the bees didn't quit.
If anything, their number increased.

Every daytime radio DJ
became an expert on bees, a bee
apologist, an apiologist.
Mothers phoned in:
a jam jar, filled with water
and a slick of jam around the edge,
that was the thing, the business, that
would bring them to their knees.
Then a keeper came on to complain,
reminding us of the differences
between wasps and bees
before going on to praise
the so-called common bee
and the Goodon's Homeless Bee, I kid you not,
as if bees were his friends ...

Which they might well have been.
It was a strange time in the world, just then,
a time of competing hypotheses,
that summer of bees.

And then one morning I awoke
to what I first thought was your clock
on the blink somewhere,
though it turned out to be,
when I snapped up the blind,
like some figure from a grainy newsreel
beamed back from the front,
just one more vulnerable creature
in a give-away uniform
having strayed too far from his unit
and across the invisible line.

Skipping

Intense as a character in a fairytale
a small girl skips in the street
outside our house. For most of the morning
she has been there, skipping and singing to herself,
now with a friend, now with a gang of friends,
at last on her own. Each time the rope comes round
she lifts herself up out of her shadow
with just a flick of her toes,
and whether friends return to chant
some muddled rhyme no small girl
ever really understands or worries about,
or whether the ice-cream van
trawls by, slows down, tinkling with promise,
on she goes, skipping and leaving the world
over and over, loving
the weight of herself, the weightlessness,
the swoosh of the rope.

War / Oil

War for oil? Oil for war?
Whatever way I look at it, I see
a newsreel image from thirty years back,
another conflict, another cursed city
of exploded homes in which the camera turns
a rubble-strewn street corner to find
the sign above one filling station
blown to HELL.

Weatherman

i.m Frank Harte (1933—2005)

When he cried, it rained.
When he sighed, the wind swelled.
When he stared into the sun, it snowed and snowed and snowed
    and snowed.
And when he closed his eyes, my weatherman, night fell.

Bread

Somewhere in a house near here
a woman lifts dough to a board on a table,
a man spreads flour with a flick of his wrist
and a child stands by with the butter and milk,
O the beating, the kneading, the rolling, the baking of bread.

The only working time machine is the smell
of warm bread cooling near a window...

Somewhere in a house near here,
set out under cover, heavy dough
begins to rise. The child begins to sing
forgotten songs. It makes her feel at home,
this beating, this kneading, this rolling, this baking of bread.

Bread baked on a fire beneath the stars,
bread expanding like the universe...

Somewhere in a house near here,
a man born in a distant land
stops a moment to dust his hands
with white flour then bends down to leave
white hand-prints on a child's dark cheeks;
they're baking bread together, while outside
an Irish garden slowly comes to life.

The journey's over, rest your weary legs,
join us now at table, share our bread.

2.

Barrel loaf, butter loaf, dinkel bread, bagel,
brotchen, ciabatta, focaccia, brioche,
cholla, challah, povatica, pretzel,
calzone, pita bread, pizza bread, batch,

ekmek from Turkey, lavosh from Armenia,
Spanish cucazarra, French baguette,
Australian damper, Russian pirog from Poland,
Rhine pumpernickel, Romanov black bread,

poblano, panettone, Polish paska, Czech
babovka and kolach, tsourekia from Greece,
hoska, hunza, sourdough, semolina,
borrowdale teabread, Scandinavian lefse,

Louisiana spoonbread, pane Pugliese,
soda bread, socca bread, Danish flatcake,
rogenbrot, volkornbrot, mandlebrot, roti,
Pan de Muertos from Mexico, the bread of the dead,

Argentinian chimichurri, Chinese steamed bunk,
hot jalapeno, snowshoe garlic naan,
Ethiopian injera, taka hallah, talladega,
filipino bibingka, Irish sliced pan.

The journey's over, rest your weary legs,
join us now at table, share our bread.

The Wonderbra Girl

She was the girl of the moment.
Eva Herzigova.
Everyone knew her name.
She was everywhere.

No journey through the city
was done until you'd seen her
stripped to her chest on a billboard,
a twinkle in each eye.

That brassiere. The way
it tugged at your attention,
pushed into every conversation,
popped up even on the news.

Motorists ignored green lights,
pedestrians walked into lampposts,
bicycles upended themselves
thanks to that girl's charms.

And not just in this city
but in cities across the globe,
the same girl's face, same bra, same pose,
spreading the way a religion does

where people meet:

weaving through the chaos
of rush-hour streets,
shoved up close together
in rush-hour queues,

and in rush-hour trains
at last heading homewards
gripping the overhead cords, blank-faced,
and swaying gently in unison.

Young Master

The community centre. Strolling past
on my way home from work one day, I hear
a body-tumbling-down-the-stairs
drum roll, then a cymbal crash.

Inside, alone on stage, a kid,
perched so high on a stool his feet
don't even reach the ground, sees
and promptly ignores me, steadying his kit

for a fresh assault. Time itself
is in a kind of trance: echoes
predict themselves, reflect themselves.
And, through the bars of light from the high, barred windows,

autumn reaches in to see
dust motes rise and swirl and bloom
as if something invisible had lifted them,
and held them now, nebulous, but free.

NOTES

'The Castlecomer Jukebox', p. 12
Thrupenny bit—three penny piece in predecimal, pre-Euro currency.

'Master', p. 19
"I am no style / and I am all styles"—Bruce Lee's description of his newly invented martial art of Jeet Kune Do which borrowed from many but was also fiercely independent of other martial arts schools or traditions.

'Coins', p. 41
Boreens are narrow roads; the word derives from the Irish word for cow, *bó,* and might literally translate as 'roads the width of a cow'.

'The Flood', p. 43
The southern county of Laois, along with its neighbour Offaly, were the two southern Irish counties planted by English settlers from 1556.

'Forest', p. 46
Dunamase is the well-known ruined castle, situated about three miles outside of Portlaoise, believed to have been destroyed by the Cromwellian colonels Hewson and Reynolds in 1650.

'I'll Do It Again', p. 58
Norma Desmond is the heroine of the movie *Sunset Boulevard* (1950) whose attempted suicide coincides with the celebration of the New Year.

'A Creation Myth', p. 105
This story of a dinner party, attended by a number of well-known physicists, at which the game of Twenty Questions was played, with unusual results, features in a number of recent science books for the general reader.

'Song of the Fish People', p. 112
The saline solution that covers the human eye is one of the last pieces of direct evidence of our evolutionary origins in salt water.

'Listening Wind', p. 123

This poem is a return to a subject that troubled me as a child: what age will we be if we should find ourselves in heaven, the age we died at or the age at which we were happiest? Will our loved ones turn out to be kids we are unlikely even to recognise? The title, for reasons I can't explain, is from a song of the same name by the band Talking Heads.

'Neighbours', p. 154

This poem is a roundabout way of recording the migration of many northern Irish families southwards during the worst years of the so-called Troubles. To a great extent, the horrors of what they had experienced on the other side of the border was entirely lost on us ill-informed southerners.

'Literature', p. 175

Rosebud is a reference to the movie *Citizen Kane* and, by extension, to the alternative or other possible life that its central character might have lived. Jekyll and Dorian Gray, similarly, refer to other fictional double existences.

'The Wheel', p. 176

The song *A Nation Once Again* by Thomas Davis (1814-1845) was widely taught to Irish schoolchildren and was therefore a regular subject for parody: Hibernation Once Again; Starvation Once Again …

'Machines', p. 181

The main building of the Royal College of Surgeons in Ireland (on York Street / St. Stephen's Green in south central Dublin), though fronted by a well-known classical facade, is for the most part an ugly and inappropriate concrete replacement for the row of Corporation flats which were demolished to accommodate it. At the time this poem is set, the corresponding second side of the street still stood, though it too has since been demolished.

Printed in the United Kingdom
by Lightning Source UK Ltd.
125356UK00001B/66/A